End Time People

Bryan Ball

The Essential Sequel to End Time Events
Timely Truth from the Epistles of Peter

Copyright © 2021 Autumn House Publications (Europe) Ltd.
Published in 2021 by Autumn House Publications (Europe) Ltd.,
Grantham, England.

All rights reserved. No part of this publication may be reproduced in any form without prior permission from the publisher.

British Library Cataloguing in Publication Data. A catalogue record for this book is available from the British Library.

Except where otherwise indicated, Scripture quotations in this book have been drawn from the New King James Version®. Copyright © 1982 by Thomas Nelson. Used by permission. All rights reserved.

Other translations used:
The Holy Bible, English Standard Version Anglicised (ESVUK). Copyright © 2001 by Crossway Bibles, a division of Good News Publishers.
The Good News Bible® (GNB): Today's English Version Second Edition, UK/British Edition. Copyright © 1992 by the British & Foreign Bible Society. Used by permission.
The King James Version (KJV). Public Domain.
The New English Bible (NEB). Copyright © by The Delegates of the Oxford University Press and The Syndics of the Cambridge University Press, 1961, 1970.
The Holy Bible, New International Version® Anglicised (NIV). Copyright © 1979, 1984, 2011 by Biblica, Inc.® Used by permission. All rights reserved worldwide.
The Holy Bible, New Living Translation (NLT). Copyright © 1996, 2004, 2015 by Tyndale House Foundation. Used by permission of Tyndale House Publishers, Inc., Carol Stream, Illinois 60188. All rights reserved.
The New Revised Standard Version: Anglicised Edition (NRSV). Copyright © 1989, 1995 by the Division of Christian Education of the National Council of the Churches of Christ in the United States of America. Used by permission. All rights reserved.
The New Testament in Modern English by J. B. Phillips. Copyright © 1960, 1972 by J. B. Phillips. Administered by The Archbishops' Council of the Church of England. Used by permission.

ISBN: 978-1-78665-916-3

Editor: David Neal
Designer: David Bell

Printed in Serbia.

End Time

Bryan Ball

People

The Essential Sequel to End Time Events
Timely Truth from the Epistles of Peter

Foreword

Bryan Ball has spent his life serving the church with distinction as a pastor, an evangelist, a scholar, administrator and writer: but, in whatever role he serves, he retains a pastor's heart. It was as my pastor that he led me to Christ. It was in the college classroom that he taught me how to be a pastor, and through the pages of *End Time People* the pastor still speaks.

With the enthusiasm of an evangelist and an unshakeable conviction in the continuing trustworthiness of Scripture, Bryan Ball draws on Peter's ancient words to speak again today. A pastor has two clear tasks – to feed the people of God with the Word of God, and to shield the people of God from error. This book accomplishes both.

Understandably, 'End Time people' want to know about 'End Time events', of which many books have been written, forensically interpreting the verses of Scripture to create an eschatological timetable. For sure, we too, like Peter, must be unambiguous that 'the end of all things is at hand' (1 Peter 4:7), and wait expectantly for His return.

Yet error is not always clear to see, often at times subtle – tipping people off balance. The case in point is that our understanding of the end times has not always made us Christ-like: clearly a concern of Peter, who asks, 'What kind of people ought you to be?' (Second Peter 3:11, NIV.) It is the core question which Bryan Ball believes will help restore balance.

To discover the direction of travel for the journey through 1 and 2 Peter, take a look at the contents page. As I scanned the chapter headings I thought, 'My life needs to be embedded in the Word. I want to be Spirit-led. To be compassionate and distinctive for the sake of Christ is surely non-negotiable?' And then I stopped and reflected on an uncomfortable truth: 'Isn't this how we all should be?'

It was the wish of Peter for his readers to 'grow in the grace and knowledge of our Lord and Saviour Jesus Christ' (2 Peter 3:18, NIV). Likewise, it is the overriding wish of the pastor who authored this book.

David Neal

Acknowledgements

Every author knows that no book can come into the hands of its readers without the assistance of many other talented people. That is as true of this book as of all others. It is, therefore, a great pleasure to express my indebtedness to those who have contributed to the publication of *End Time People*, most of them unknown to me by name. They include the Administrative Committee at the Stanborough Press, the Editorial Reading Committee, the proof-reader (Andrew Puckering), the design and layout artist (David Bell), cost managers, marketing and publicity agents, and of course the entire production team at the Adventist publishing house in Serbia. Without any of them this book could never have become a reality.

There are two in particular whose names I do know and have done for many years, and who deserve special mention. David Neal is the best editor I have ever worked with, and there have been many. His enthusiasm for the project has been evident from the time he first read the manuscript in its initial form. He has consistently been a very perceptive and sensitive critic and a good communicator; and his support through difficult times, when I wondered if the book would ever be finished, has been a great encouragement.

The other person I have known even longer, for more than sixty years in fact, before she became my wife. Dawn too has been a constant support, as she has on many occasions, and her keen eye for details such as punctuation and spelling errors, ambiguities and inconsistencies, as well as places in the text which needed clarification, has materially improved the final version. She has carefully read every chapter, some more than once, and they have all been improved by her observations. She has on previous occasions requested that her name not be mentioned, so I didn't ask her this time! I may need to ask forgiveness.

When my last book was published in 2015, I wrote in the foreword, 'While I cannot say that this will be my last book, it is also a grateful acknowledgement of a long and rewarding life.' My feelings remain the same, but I suspect that Father Time could have something to do with the final outcome.

So my very sincere thanks go to all mentioned above, and to any who may unintentionally have been overlooked. You have all helped make this book a reality. It was written from a deep conviction of a great and urgent need in the Church, and also in the world to which the Church has been called to bear witness, living as we do at this critical and unprecedented time in Earth's history. Under God's blessing, may it accomplish its purpose.

Bryan Ball
Cooranbong, New South Wales, Australia

July 2021

Also by Bryan Ball
A Great Expectation
The English Connection
The Seventh-day Men
Living in the Spirit
Can We Still Believe the Bible?
The Essential Jesus (ed.)
The Soul Sleepers
In the Beginning (ed.)
Grounds for Assurance and Faith

Contributor to
The Encyclopedia of World Faiths
The Advent Hope in Scripture and History
The Oxford Dictionary of National Biography
The Development of Pluralism in Modern Britain and France
Exploring the Frontiers of Faith
The Book that Changed the World
The Oxford Dictionary of the Christian Church (advisor)

Contents

Chapter 1
End Time People 8

Chapter 2
An Alien People 20

Chapter 3
Christian People 31

Chapter 4
People of the Word 42

Chapter 5
Spirit-led People 53

Chapter 6
Thinking People... 64

Chapter 7
Redeemed People 74

Chapter 8
Born-again People.. 85

Chapter 9
People who Grow 96

Chapter 10
People with Faith 108

Chapter 11
Compassionate People................................. 120

Chapter 12
Distinctive People....................................... 132

Chapter 13
Steadfast People 144

Chapter 14
People who Hope 155

Chapter 15
People who Witness.................................... 167

Chapter 16
The End Time 178

Appendix: Sources 192

End Time People

1

This book has been written to bring some necessary balance to what, in the writer's opinion, has often been an unbalanced emphasis on last-day events. It is also an attempt to understand what it means to live in the time of the end, particularly as Peter understood it. There is, of course, nothing wrong with wanting to understand Bible prophecy and what it says about the last days. In fact, it is necessary to do so. Sadly, it is one of the characteristics of much of contemporary Christianity that it says little if anything about the great prophecies of the Bible and the last days. The result is an anaemic and largely impotent church which seems irrelevant in the secular world to which it is supposed to witness. The Adventist emphasis on biblical prophecy has brought understanding and new meaning to the lives of untold thousands across the world. I have preached on last-day events myself – but not always, as I have since come to realise, with the balance necessary to a full and healthy understanding of what it means to live in the last days and what it means to be ready for the Lord's return. It is easy enough to forget that Jesus said to His disciples, 'Be ready, for the Son of Man is coming at an hour you do not expect'

> **Being ready is more important than knowing the time of the end.**

(Matthew 24:44). Being ready is more important than knowing the time of the end.

The American historian Perry Miller, in his book *Errand into the Wilderness*, illustrates what can happen to individuals and to society itself when there are unbalanced beliefs about future events. Between the years 1755 and 1758 there was a growing conviction that Halley's comet was on a collision course with earth and that the end of the world was at hand. Churches began to fill; people began to pray and read their Bibles. As the time drew near, religious fervour intensified. But 1758 came and went, and the comet did not arrive as predicted. Miller describes the result when people realised that Halley's comet had let them off:

> 'Great numbers went together to the Taverns and broke up whole Hogsheads for joy. . . . They Drank, they Whored, they Swore, they Lied, they Cheated, they Plunder'd, they Gam'd, they Quarrell'd, they Murder'd. In short, the World went on in the Old Channel.'

Miller draws a very significant lesson from this fiasco: 'People cannot be scared into virtue.' There was no inner moral or spiritual imperative to require a virtuous life. It is a lesson that many in more recent times have been slow to learn. Mere knowledge of events, real or conjectured, present or future or for that matter past, cannot of itself result in changed lives.

As its title indicates, this book seeks to correct this imbalance. An understanding of End Time events must be accompanied by the recognition that such knowledge is only useful if it leads to authentic End Time people. Understanding and lifestyle are, in true Christian experience, inseparably related. The purpose of this book is to explain how and why, particularly in Peter's epistles, this connection is deemed necessary and experientially possible. It will, I believe, be an enlightening and enjoyable experience. But, before we come to the text itself, two underlying questions must first be answered. Can Peter's belief that he was writing in the last days to people who lived in the first century be substantiated? And, if so, is it also valid to claim that what he wrote then is equally relevant to the Church today? The remainder of this chapter attempts to answer these two questions. The chapters which follow fill in the details and paint a picture of the kind of people Peter believes End Time people should be. It should be noted that throughout this book the terms 'last days', 'end time', and 'time of the end' are used synonymously unless otherwise stated.

> This anticipated salvation is now 'ready to be revealed'. Its time has come. It is urgent for us to be ready.

There cannot be any question that Peter's epistles were written to early Christian believers in the conviction that both writer and readers were living in the last days. The first epistle begins with a reminder that believers are kept by the power of God as they wait for their salvation, to be revealed 'in the last time' (1 Peter 1:5). The New English Bible and the Good News Bible translate this phrase, 'at the end of time'. This anticipated salvation is now 'ready to be revealed'. Its time has come. It is urgent for us to be ready. In verse 20 of this same chapter Peter writes specifically of 'these last times', which the New English Bible translates as 'this last period of time' and the New Revised Standard Version as 'at the end of the ages'.

Peter's belief that he is writing about the last days and to people living in those days is put beyond all doubt when he declares unambiguously, 'The end of all things is at hand' (1 Peter 4:7). Writing in the *Tyndale New Testament Commentary,* Wayne Grudem explains the meaning of this text as it relates to God's plan of redemption and the salvation that is now 'ready to be revealed'. In the long sequence of events leading up to the coming of the Saviour, beginning with Creation and the Fall, and ending in the return of Christ at the last day, Grudem states:

> The end of all things is at hand.

> *'The end of all things is at hand* means that all the major events in God's plan of redemption have occurred, and now all things are ready for Christ to return and rule. The great "last act", the church age, had been continuing for about thirty years by the time Peter wrote. Thus the curtain could fall at any time, ushering in the return of Christ and the

end of the age. All things are ready: *the end of all things* (the goal to which all these events have been leading) *is at hand.'*

Even a cursory reading of Peter's first epistle conveys the fact that he is convinced that he and all those to whom he was writing were living at the end of time. They were literally End Time people.

It is necessary to pause here and note carefully that Peter's emphasis on the last days *is in harmony with other New Testament statements* which state that the early Christian church mid-way through the first century AD was living at the end of time. In the epistle to the Romans, Paul reminds them, in words similar to those Peter uses, 'Now our salvation is nearer than when we first believed. The night is far spent, the day is at hand' (Romans 13:11, 12). Paul writes to the Corinthians about things that occurred in Old Testament times 'to warn us who live at the end of the age' (1 Corinthians 10:11, NLT). The author of Hebrews begins his epistle by saying that God 'has in these last days spoken to us by His Son' (Hebrews 1:1, 2). John, writing nearer the end of the first century, puts it even more dramatically: 'It is the last hour; and as you have heard that the Antichrist is coming, even now many antichrists have come, by which we know that it is the last hour' (1 John 2:18). Christians at this time believed that a great enemy of God and the Church, known as the Antichrist, would appear before Christ's return. His appearance was proof that this was indeed the 'last hour', the last of the last days. Peter is in good company when he writes to End Time people about those days.

Some have questioned how the writers of the New Testament can so consistently refer to their days as the last days when now, two millennia later, Christians still read the same things and apply them to the twenty-first century. It is a good question, and there is a good answer. It is directly related to the salvation Peter says is *ready to be revealed* in the last days, and to how we understand the word 'salvation' and the term 'last days'. Does salvation mean only what happened at Calvary; a synonym, perhaps, for redemption?

In his book, *The Jesus Hope,* Stephen Travis places Jesus at the very heart of historic Christian belief and future hope, and explains that salvation includes everything Jesus was, did and will do: not only what took place on the cross, vital though that unquestionably is. He further explains that the last days are the entire time between the resurrection of Jesus and His second coming. This whole period is called in the Bible 'the last days'. Travis says, 'They are not the final few years before the return of Jesus, but the whole period from Jesus' resurrection to His final coming, however long that may be.' That is why Peter can say salvation is ready to be revealed 'at the end of time' (1 Peter 1:5, NEB and GNB), or 'on the last day' (NLT).

> Does salvation mean only what happened at Calvary; a synonym, perhaps, for redemption?

This long period between the two comings of Christ has been called 'The Christ Event', meaning not merely His birth, death, resurrection, or priestly ministry in heaven, but everything He was and said and did. The 'Christ Event' will not be over until He comes again and the victory over sin and death and evil is finally won. Speaking of the great conflict between good and evil now being played out on earth, Travis adds that although through His life and death 'Christ won the victory in principle at His first coming, the victory will not be complete until His return'. Writing extensively about the kingdom of God, John Bright says, 'The promised victory, although it could not be doubted, was clearly not complete,' adding: 'That victory was not doubted, but eagerly and imminently expected. The early church felt that it was living in the last days and that time was short.' The Dutch theologian Berkouwer comments on the time between the two comings of Christ, describing it as the 'already' and the 'not yet'.

A more scholarly work, *The Parousia in The New Testament,* by A. L. Moore, examines at great length the end-time expectation prevalent throughout the New Testament, *parousia* being the Greek word for 'coming'. Moore says it means 'that the End is near . . . it might come at any moment', commenting on 'the readiness of the End to break in to the present order'. On Hebrews 1:2 and 10 he speaks of 'the approaching Day', referring to the 'hope that this may occur soon' and that 'it is not far distant'. Moore concludes his enlightening study of the New Testament evidence on a note very similar to the views of Stephen Travis and John Bright.

In view of all this it is impossible to doubt that much of the New Testament, including the epistles of Peter, was written to the early church under the conviction that the End Time had come. They were living in the last days, waiting for their salvation to be finally and fully revealed. Some of this may be new to some readers, but it may help to remember that it explains why we are still here.

> They were living in the last days, waiting for their salvation to be finally and fully revealed.

With this background, we may now return to Peter. As noted, everything he writes in his first epistle is written in the unshakeable conviction that he and those who would read that letter and hear it read were living at the end of time. Yet, remarkably, he says nothing about the signs of the times or the fulfilment of prophecy. These are not on his agenda, and we will shortly see why. Only when he comes to the last chapter of the second epistle does Peter describe the last days, and then he writes forcefully about the 'scoffers' who will come and the false doctrines they will proclaim. He then presses home his main point, asking what might today be called the 'million-dollar question' – the big one, the all-important question that cannot be avoided by any who claim to live in the last days, at the very end of time.

> ... he says nothing about the signs of the times or the fulfilment of prophecy. These are not on his agenda, and we will shortly see why.

The context of this question must not be overlooked. It is the appearance of the scoffers Peter describes in the previous verses. He says they 'deliberately forget' the truths of God's word, turning a blind eye to the evidence and saying, 'Where is this "coming" he promised? Ever since our ancestors died, everything goes on as it has since the beginning of creation' (2 Peter 3:3, 4, NIV). Such scoffers still exist today. I met one of them at an interdenominational conference in the 1970s.

Delegates to the conference had all been assigned to discussion groups to bring recommendations to the main assembly on how the Church could respond to the rising tide of secularism. At what I felt was an appropriate point I brought up the question of Christ's second coming. It went down like a lead balloon. I can still remember the incredulity in the chairman's voice as he said, 'You don't really believe that, do you?' I replied that there were many thinking Christians who believed it, and that their point of view should not be simply dismissed as irrelevant. Clearly, he was not impressed. He was a 'modernist', an 'enlightened' member of Christ's contemporary church who had left behind what they considered to be an outdated theology, replacing it with a more recent and 'credible' way of interpreting the Bible. Reading the opening verses of 2 Peter 3 in the context of the preceding chapters, it is clear that Peter knew that similar views already existed in the Church in his day, pointing out that they were deceptive and dangerous.

> 'Therefore, since all these things will be dissolved, what manner of persons ought you to be in holy conduct and godliness?'

In the light of that sobering reality and the possibility that some were already wavering in their belief, forgetful of the things they had learned when they first believed, Peter stresses the validity of the apostolic faith and the certainty of Christ's return. He then asks the 'million-dollar question' – the one that should be uppermost in the thinking of all End Time people. With an unmistakable reference to Jesus' own words about the last days, Peter says:

'The day of the Lord will come as a thief in the night, in which the heavens will pass away with a great noise, and the elements will melt with fervent heat; both the earth and the works that are in it will be burned up. Therefore, since all these things will be dissolved, *what manner of persons ought you to be in holy conduct and godliness?*' (2 Peter 3:10, 11, emphasis supplied.)

The NIV translation reads, 'What kind of people ought you to be?' The reply is equally pointed: 'You ought to live holy and godly lives. . . .' That might seem to be a perfectly good answer, succinctly describing End Time people. It appears to be quite adequate. So why don't we leave it there? Because there is another way of looking at both the question and the answer recorded in 2 Peter 3:10, 11.

A question is often asked at the beginning of an article or a book to catch the attention of readers, hoping to engage them in thinking of possible answers. In this instance the question comes at the end of Peter's epistles, and the briefest of answers is given immediately. It would normally take an entire book to answer adequately a question of this magnitude, especially if the writer were not restricted to the letters of Peter, as is the case in this book. Could it be possible, then, that Peter asks the question here, not at the beginning by way of introduction, but at the end by way of conclusion, *because he knows that he has already answered it in the previous seven and a half chapters of his epistles?* The brief answer given here in verse 11 may be regarded as a succinct summary of everything he has previously said about living in the end time, all leading to the conclusion, 'You ought to live holy and godly lives.' Peter is saying, in effect, 'Read these chapters for yourselves; study them carefully, think about them . . . and you will discover what kind of people End Time people really are.'

In all probability, that is what he would be saying today if he had known he was writing to twenty-first-century Christians as well as to those who lived at the beginning of Christian history. It cannot be overstated that Peter's epistles are as much for Christians today as they were to Christians in the first century. We should read them with that in mind. We are living in the End Time, just as they were, in the expectation of Christ's soon return, when the great 'Christ Event' of the centuries comes to its final triumphant conclusion. Concerning 1 Peter, Grudem says, 'I do not think that any Christian can study this letter . . . without hearing in it the voice of God speaking powerfully to the needs of today's church.'

Finally, a few words by way of explanation. This book is not a traditional word-by-word, chapter-by-chapter commentary on Peter's epistles. It is not a theological exposition based on a detailed understanding of the original Greek, but rather a pastoral commentary in which Peter's concerns for the life of the Church and its members are spelt out. Peter is primarily concerned more about who we are than what we believe. These are letters, not doctrinal treatises, as were some of the other books of the New Testament such as Romans, Galatians or Hebrews, which were written specifically to deal with issues of doctrine or interpretation which had appeared in some places and which required clarification or outright rebuttal. It is true of course that 2 Peter 2 does consider this issue; but, even so, it is written from a pastoral perspective, as verse 1 of that chapter makes clear. So the truths that Peter sets out are explained in this book with the aid of appropriate illustrations, personal experiences, relevant quotations, historical events, poetry and the words of well-known hymns, as well as simple explanations of the original Greek words Peter uses. In that respect I have tried to remember – frequently with little success, I fear – Hugh Dunton's classic one-liner on biblical interpretation: 'It is of little value to go down deep if we come up dry.'

For those who would like to delve more deeply into some of the things Peter says, much can be gained from Wayne Grudem's commentary on 1 Peter in the *Tyndale New Testament Commentary* series and from Michael Green's commentary on 2 Peter in the same series. Edmund Clowney's *The Message of 1 Peter*, in a series edited by John Stott, is also helpful. William Barclay's commentary on Peter's epistles in *The Daily Study Bible* remains as popular as ever, and Lenski's older commentary never fails to bring something new to our attention.

Our approach to Peter's letters, then, will be a thematic approach, picking up what he says about a relevant topic wherever it appears in the text. This means we will move to and fro in the epistles to bring together everything Peter says on any given subject – salvation, obedience, holiness, the new birth, for example – anything he believes adds to the understanding and daily living of End Time people. This may not seem a very good way to approach any part of the Bible, but we remember that these are letters, not treatises. It should also be noted that Peter assumes that some of the things he mentions are so foundational to the Christian message that it is not necessary to go over them again in detail. So he refers to them only once, moving on to his special concerns – satisfied that his readers, all recently converted, are sufficiently grounded in the basic essentials of their new faith.

Peter's epistles, then, were written to express Peter's concern for the life of the Church and to help all believers to live a full and satisfying life in Christ. In the chapters that follow we will attempt to grasp just what that entails, hoping to discover the main essentials of Peter's message to the Church. In doing this, we will not be concerned with some of the details. There will be large chunks of the text that we will pass over in the attempt to capture the big picture, to ascertain Peter's central message. We will discover, I believe, that, in describing what kind of people End Time people should be, Peter answers clearly the 'million-dollar' question. Perhaps the best summary of Peter's purposes comes at the end of the first epistle where he explains why he has written the letter. It is to 'perfect, establish, strengthen, and settle you ... exhorting and testifying that this is the true grace of God in which you stand' (1 Peter 5:10, 12). Clowney correctly comments, 'Peter describes the power of that grace in four verbs: God will complete His work in us; He will establish us, strengthen us and ground us.'

Peter's great burden for all End Time people – then and now – is that, through the working of God within, they will be established in the faith, and that God's work of grace will be completed in them and in the Church. They will understand what living in the End Time really means and what it requires. They will not only assent to Christian teaching, vital as that unquestionably is, but they will also understand and experience the wonderful love of God, ever growing 'in the grace and knowledge of our Lord and Savior Jesus Christ'

> End Time events will be accompanied and adorned by End Time people, ready and waiting for the Lord's return.

(2 Peter 3:18). End Time events will be accompanied and adorned by End Time people, ready and waiting for the Lord's return – not necessarily living carbon copies of each other's lives, but all nonetheless characterised by the qualities Peter describes.

Many readers may have heard or read this little poem before, but it will bear repetition since it expresses vividly the journey, the hope and the reward of real End Time people:

We are near to the end of the journey;
We have come to earth's crisis hour,
When love shall be crowned with glory,
And justice stand up in power;
When the forces of wrong, defeated,
Shall cease with the setting sun;
And the last great page of this mighty age
Sends forth its decree, 'It is done.'

We are near to the end of the journey,
No time now to loiter or wait;
So close to the kingdom of glory,
So nigh to the heavenly gate;
The Daystar divine has arisen,
Though dark was the pathway we trod.
We soon shall abide with the glorified
In the paradise of God.

End Time people from every age of history and from every nation and culture in the world have experienced the grace of God, have lived in the light of the approaching end, and have looked forward to the final reward of the saints. That's what Peter's epistles will tell us again . . . and they will, I believe, confirm our faith and our hope.

For reflection and further study

1. Why is 'being ready' more important than knowing the time of the end?
2. How does 1 Peter 3:10, 11 answer this question?
3. Do you think there is a difference between 'being ready' and 'getting ready'?

2 An Alien People

'Peter, an apostle of Jesus Christ, to the pilgrims of the Dispersion in Pontus, Galatia, Cappadocia, Asia, and Bithynia' (1 Peter 1:1). Originally written to Christians inhabiting the areas of Asia Minor named here, this opening verse of Peter's first epistle might be thought of little consequence to the rest of the letter – hardly more than a salutation, perhaps, after the way in which most of the New Testament epistles begin. That would be a great mistake, for in these few words Peter lays down two fundamentally important principles which undergird the whole epistle, and only in the light of which can everything Peter says be fully understood.

He first establishes his credentials by clarifying his identity: 'Peter, an apostle of Jesus Christ'. Apostolic authority would be important to the 'scattered' people throughout Asia Minor who would read this epistle or hear it read. Some of them, particularly those in the more rural areas, may not even have heard of him, since he was writing thirty years or so after the birth of Christianity in Jerusalem, and since most of the churches in the regions mentioned in verse 1 had been established by Paul. This is not to imply any preference for Paul over Peter in these churches, but to note that during his second and third missionary journeys, c. AD 46-57, Paul had travelled throughout Asia Minor, ten to fifteen years before Peter wrote his first epistle c. AD 64, and had established and consolidated many of these churches. It would have been only natural for those early believers to regard Paul as their father in the faith. For these reasons it was necessary for them to be satisfied that Peter was writing with a divine mandate, and that what he wrote was authoritative and acceptable to the whole church. William Barclay remarks that when Peter's letters were being written 'there was an outbreak of letter-writing in the Church'. Some of these letters have survived, but not as part of the New Testament, as have the epistles of Peter. It is understandable that Peter wanted to assure his readers that he was a *bona fide* 'apostle of Jesus Christ'.

Having first established his credentials, he now establishes his credibility. The regions listed in verse 1 were known geographical and administrative areas of Asia Minor in the Roman Empire. Churches had been established in all of them well before the end of the first century AD, although they would not be tolerated by Rome for nearly another three centuries, until the emperor Constantine recognised Christianity as an official religion of the Roman Empire c. AD 313. It can confidently be said, however, that a network of churches existed throughout Asia Minor by about the middle of the first century AD. The places were real; the churches were real; the people who lived there and worshipped in the churches were real. This was no *Alice in Wonderland* story. Everything Peter said so succinctly in verse 1 was true, and when people read what Peter had written at the beginning of his epistle it gave them the assurance that what he had written in the rest of the epistle was equally credible. It is not difficult to see that Peter's credentials and his credibility were of immense importance to the church of his day, as indeed they still are to us today.

It is also important to note that the epistle was written in a time of persecution, as can be seen at several points in the text.

Barclay cites E. J. Goodspeed, who wrote, 'First Peter is one of the most moving pieces of persecution literature,' commenting, 'It is written out of the love of a pastor's heart to help people who were going through it and on whom worse things were still to come.' He concludes, 'To this day it is one of the easiest letters in the New Testament to read, for it has never lost its winsome appeal to the human heart.'

> They don't belong here. They are just passing through. Their eyes are fixed on a better land, and a better future.

Before we leave the first verse of chapter one, there is a further question: 'For whom was this epistle initially written?' The answer to this question is probably the most important truth in 1 Peter 1:1. The NKJV states that the epistle was written specifically 'to the pilgrims of the Dispersion' living in the various territories of Asia Minor, now Turkey. The 'Dispersion' took place soon after the day of Pentecost when early Christians were scattered across the world following the persecution of believers in and around Jerusalem. The key word in this text is 'pilgrims'. It brings to mind, perhaps, the Pilgrim Fathers who left England in 1620, bound for the New World, to escape persecution for their faith in the countries of their birth. 'Pilgrims' is the translation of the Greek word *parepidemos*, meaning 'stranger', or 'transient resident'.

This word has many shades of meaning, as is evident from the many different renderings in modern English translations. The difference in these various versions is worth noting, as it illustrates the richness of the word and the difficulty in translating it precisely:
- *The New International Version*: 'exiles, scattered'
- *English Standard Version*: 'exiles of the Dispersion'
- *The Good News Bible*: 'refugees'
- *The New Living Translation*: 'foreigners'
- *The New American Standard Bible*: 'those who reside as strangers'

Edmund Clowney translates the phrase as 'alien residents in a foreign place', and Wayne Grudem supports the 1995 edition of the New American Standard Bible's translation of *parepidemos*, which also uses the word 'aliens'. The marginal alternative in the NKJV of the phrase 'the time of your stay' in 1 Peter 1:17 is 'sojourning', or 'dwelling as resident aliens'. Barclay says that the 'pilgrims' are 'scattered as exiles throughout' the regions of Asia Minor, commenting: 'They take their share of all responsibilities as citizens, and endure all disabilities as aliens. Every foreign land is their native land, and every native land a foreign land . . . they pass their days upon earth, but their citizenship is in heaven.' There is good reason to believe that 'alien' is an appropriate word to describe End Time people. They don't belong here. They are just passing through. Their eyes are fixed on a better land, and a better future.

In our time the word 'alien' has acquired a new meaning, one that is somewhat at odds with the biblical meaning. Since the release of the movie *E.T. The Extra-Terrestrial* in 1982, an alien is not quite what it used to be. Acclaimed as one of the greatest films of all time, its influence was incalculable. It is the story of an extra-terrestrial, E.T., stranded out in the universe three million light years from home on a distant planet. Ronald and Nancy Reagan were moved by it, and Princess Diana is said to have been in tears after watching it. 'Alien' has unfortunately taken on the meaning of a little green man from outer space who has landed on earth near a service station and marched up to a fuel pump, menacingly demanding, 'Take me to your leader.' An alien in the popular mind is not human. He is from elsewhere in the universe, and has long legs and arms, a thin body and a small, pointed head. We may smile at the imagery, but even this concept of 'alien' retains a central truth. An alien is 'out of this world'; he does not belong here. In this sense a Christian is an alien, 'in the world, but not of the world', if we read 1 John 2:15-17 correctly:

> 'Do not love the world or the things in the world. If anyone loves the world, the love of the Father is not in him. For all that is in the world – the lust of the flesh, the lust of the eyes, and the pride of life – is not of the Father but is of the world. And the world is passing away, and the lust of it; but he who does the will of God abides forever.'

John wrote this thirty years or so after Peter had written his first epistle, yet Peter might just as well have written it himself, for no one was more sure than he that the world was passing away and that End Time people should live in the light of that impending reality.

The burning question is: 'How?' How can Christians live as aliens in a foreign land? How can they be 'in the world but not of the world'? To live as aliens in a distant land is not as easy as it may sound, but the question must be faced and must be answered. Peter's first letter was written chiefly to supply the answer, which begins in verse 2: 'chosen according to the foreknowledge of God the Father, through the sanctifying work of the Spirit, to be obedient to Jesus Christ' (NIV). There are three key assertions here which undergird the entire epistle, reminding us today, as well as first-century Christians, of our status and obligations as believers.

The chosen people of God

It will not be out of place to note at this point that this text indicates that first-century Christians were Trinitarian, ascribing specific functions to each Person of the Godhead, all of whom have a part in the work of salvation, which Peter comes to shortly. This, however, is not Peter's first concern. Most of all he wants the readers of this letter to remember who they are and what they are – chosen people. Living constantly in the face of ostracism and persecution, it would have been easy to wonder if God had forgotten them; so here, at the beginning of a letter which speaks often of trials and persecution, Peter reminds them that they are chosen, the 'elect'. They are, in fact, even more than that. They are 'a chosen generation, a royal priesthood, a holy nation, His own special people' (1 Peter 2:9). These first-century Christians had replaced the people of Israel as God's own.

Speaking of God's people in Old Testament times, Clowney says:

'They are God's inheritance, His personal and prized possession, His treasure. God bears them on His shoulder, carries them in His arms, holds them in His hand, seats them at His feet. He loves them with a jealous love . . . they bear His name.'

Peter applies all this to God's new Israel. What an immeasurably elevated status this was, and what great encouragement it would have been to all who heard it as they lived out their lives in an increasingly uncertain and perilous world.

> 'We have the honour of being specially chosen by God,' he says, 'but there is also a challenge and a responsibility here.'

We need not digress here to discuss the foreknowledge of God. For one thing, it would take too long to deal with adequately. Suffice it to say that much ink has been spilt through the centuries in attempting to prove or disprove the predestinarian convictions of those with a strong Calvinistic heritage. For another thing, Peter himself does not go down this road, and for another we can be absolutely sure that God knows what He is doing. Barclay applies this to all later Christians, including those living in the twenty-first century, as Peter surely would have approved. 'We have the honour of being specially chosen by God,' he says, 'but there is also a challenge and a responsibility here.' This fundamental reality is one of the keys to understanding Peter's letters. The immensity of this reality flows in particular throughout 1 Peter: sometimes as seen here in chapter 1 verse 2; sometimes unseen, but nonetheless relevant to Peter's chief concern, as he explains what it means to live as 'aliens' in a foreign land.

Changed people

Peter continues, 'through the sanctifying work of the Spirit'. Leaving aside for the moment the work of the Spirit in sanctification, which will be considered in a later chapter, the key word in this phrase is 'sanctification' itself. It is translated from the Greek *hagiasmos*, which means 'being set apart', or 'becoming holy'. The dictionary definition of the verb 'sanctify' is 'to consecrate' or 'to set apart as holy'. There is a subtle but important difference between being consecrated, or set apart, and being holy. Sanctification in the sense of 'consecration' indicates being set apart without any moral or spiritual change within. Church buildings and graveyards, even church dignitaries, can be consecrated in this sense, but without any inner change or renewal.

Perhaps this is why many modern versions of the Bible, including the Good News Bible, the New Living Translation and J. B. Phillips' New Testament in Modern English, use the words 'holy' or 'holiness' instead of 'sanctification' in translating 1 Peter 1:2. The NLT says 'made you holy' and the GNB refers to a 'holy people'. They are not only 'set apart'. They are, or are in the process of becoming, different people, holy people. The dictionary definition of 'holy' is 'morally or spiritually excellent'. Such people are different. They have been changed. Many Bible dictionaries or word books do not have a separate entry for 'sanctify' or 'sanctification', but merely advise: 'See "Holy".' It cannot be doubted that sanctification as it has been traditionally understood has in it a sense of holiness or inner renewal, which Peter alludes to frequently throughout his first epistle. His concern is to emphasise that End Time people are now different from the people they once were. Aliens in a foreign land do not have the same concerns or live as do the native inhabitants.

Yet sanctification in the sense of being 'set apart' without connotations of inner renewal has frequently been preferred by some Christians, as it still is today. It is not hard to see why. Continual emphasis on holiness as the goal of Christian living, especially for End Time people, can easily lead to the idea that sinless perfection is essential for sanctification to be complete. It is a serious error. Those who urge us to 'be like Jesus' should explain what they mean. He was the sinless Lamb of God, the only One in human history to have lived a life without sin. If we could be like Jesus, we would not need Him. Sanctification, correctly understood, is indeed an essential reality in the Christian life. It leads to holiness, but never to perfection. Peter, therefore, reminds his readers that, having been designated as God's new Israel, they are now a holy priesthood and a holy nation (1 Peter 2:5, 9).

> **Such people are different. They have been changed.**

J. M. Furness, in his book *Vital Words of the Bible*, refers to several New Testament texts and points out that Christians are frequently called 'the holy ones' or 'saints', saying, 'Holiness is not required only of a few specialists in religion; it is demanded by Christ of all who belong to Him.' He then says, and it is a point we should not miss, 'All holiness is derived – things and people are holy only as they are near Him who is holy.'

A sanctified or holy person is therefore a saint, in the true biblical meaning of that word. It does not mean a godly person who has now departed this life and is now living in heaven, or one who goes to extraordinary lengths to show his saintliness while still on earth. A remarkable case of the latter is that of Simeon Stylites, a fifth-century ascetic who spent thirty-seven years of his life living fifteen metres above the ground on a small platform at the top of a stone column near Aleppo in Syria. We cannot know all his motives for such extreme behaviour, but if one of them was to be nearer heaven and therefore to be nearer God, he was going in the right direction, if not by the right means. A more recent instance of this noble aspiration is that expressed in Sarah Adams' lovely hymn, 'Nearer, my God, to Thee', reputed to have been played by the band of the *Titanic* as she was sinking in the Atlantic in 1912. Both these stories illustrate in different ways Peter's great concern for holiness in End Time people – as always, only derived from being 'near Him who is holy'.

> 'All holiness is derived – things and people are holy only as they are near Him who is holy.'

Called to obedience
Ever since the Reformation, there have been Christians who have been reluctant to endorse the concept of obedience. It sounds to them too much like salvation by works. Some were then, and some still are, known as 'antinomians'. The word comes from two Greek words: *anti*, meaning 'against', and *nomos*, meaning 'law'. They were against keeping the law, particularly the Ten Commandments, for fear of falling into legalism. Clearly, they were unaware of Peter's teaching about obedience, to say nothing of the teaching of the rest

of the New Testament, which confirms Peter's emphasis.

Peter first uses the word in 1 Peter 1:2, according to the NKJV, in a rather obscure phrase: 'for obedience and sprinkling of the blood of Jesus Christ'. It seems that obedience is in some way related to Christ's blood or His death. The NIV and NRSV are clearer, the former giving 'to be obedient to Jesus Christ', and the latter 'to be obedient to Jesus Christ and to be sprinkled with his blood'. If we link this to Peter's reference to obedience in verse 22, 'obeying the truth', we have the basis for Christian obedience, as opposed to the obedience of the Jew, regulated by a law composed of rules and regulations. Grudem says, commenting on 1 Peter 1:2:

> 'Peter's readers, of course, realised that their obedience in this life was always incomplete, that even the most mature Christians were painfully aware of remaining sin, and that God's purpose, "obedience to Jesus Christ", would never be completely fulfilled in this life.'

It should be noted that Peter uses the word 'obedient' again in verse 14, after already referring to salvation three times (1 Peter 1:5, 9, 10). The danger of legalism can only arise once salvation has been understood and received. The issue then, as now, is whether or not Christians should keep the Ten Commandments in view of the fact that they are 'not under law but under grace' (Romans 6:15). Bypassing for now the necessity of interpreting this oft-quoted text correctly, it is not yielding the field to concede that determining the truth about law and grace is somewhat like walking a tightrope, where keeping one's balance is essential to survival.

In 1954 Professor J. N. D. Anderson delivered the presidential address entitled 'Law and Grace' at the Inter-Varsity Conference in London, pointing out that it seemed to him to be 'unusually easy to be woolly-minded' about the matter, 'with great damage not only to the understanding, but to the whole spiritual life'. In 1964 Dr Ernest Kevan, principal of London Bible College, published a fine study on the subject with the title *Keep His Commandments: The Place of Law in the Christian Life*. In it he explained in detail the biblical teaching about law and grace, stressing the ongoing obligation of Christians to observe the moral law as set down in the Ten Commandments. These two publications alone are still sufficient to demonstrate that there is fundamentally no conflict between law and grace, and that from a biblical standpoint the obedience of love is a logical and necessary consequence of the Gospel. Law and grace are not incompatible. They are, in fact, inseparable.

Peter understood this; and, in the context of their newly-found salvation, he writes to his early Christian readers as 'obedient children' who have 'purified [their] souls in obeying the truth through the Spirit' (1 Peter 1:14, 22). He also warns of disobedience, which is a cause of 'stumbling', leading to ungodliness and ultimately to death and the loss of salvation (1 Peter 2:8; 3:20; 2 Peter 2:5-8). Grudem, again, says that when Peter uses the word 'obedience' he refers to 'the daily obedience of believers', an obligation in harmony with Paul's use of the word – for example, in Romans 6:16 and 2 Corinthians 2:9 and 7:15. Dr Kevan sums it all up neatly and clearly:

Law and grace are not incompatible. They are, in fact, inseparable.

> 'The Ten Commandments are valid for all men everywhere and for all time; they are absolute and admit of no historical or geographical limitation. . . . If the experience of the grace of God has any influence at all on the believer's obligation to fulfil the Law of God, it is rather to increase that obligation than to diminish it.'

Isaac Watts saw it from another equally valid perspective when he wrote in that much-loved hymn, 'When I Survey the Wondrous Cross': 'Love so amazing, so divine, demands my soul, my life, my all.'

'Love so amazing, so divine, demands my soul, my life, my all.'

How, then, should End Time people live, aliens and sojourners as they are in a foreign land? They should constantly remember that they are God's own chosen people, His elect. They should live daily in the pursuit of holiness, however difficult at times it may seem; and they should let that all be seen by their willingness to live in obedience to the revealed will of God. When we come to the end of verse 2 of 1 Peter 1, a solid foundation has been laid for all that follows in the rest of the epistle.

For reflection and further study

1. Imagine what it must have been like to be a Christ-follower living in the first century AD.
2. Consider the tension between the joy of believing in the resurrected Christ, and the fear of a knock on the door from the civil authorities.

Christian People 3

It might be thought unnecessary for Peter to point out that the early believers to whom he was writing were Christians. Were they not already aware of that? Were they not prepared to suffer for their faith, as Christ had suffered for them? Yet there is a strong indication in 2 Peter 2 that there was substantial cause for Peter to be concerned enough to remind them of their allegiance to Christ; since by AD 64, when this letter was written, that allegiance had already been challenged. Peter wrote in his second letter, as translated in the NIV:

'There will be false teachers among you. They will secretly introduce destructive heresies, even denying the sovereign Lord who bought them. . . . Many will follow their depraved conduct and will bring the way of truth into disrepute' (2 Peter 2:1, 2).

There appears to be a link here to something Paul says in 2 Corinthians 11:4, which was written ten years or so before 2 Peter, where Paul refers to those who preach 'another Jesus' and 'a different gospel' to that which the Corinthians had first

What Peter said about Jesus is just as important for twenty-first-century Christians as it was for those who lived in the first century – perhaps even more so.

31

accepted. Whether or not Peter knew of that epistle, he warns the recently converted Christians of Asia Minor, in strong terms that cannot be misunderstood, of false teachers and insidious heresies which deny 'the sovereign Lord who bought them'. Since the first and foremost mark of an authentic Christian is allegiance to the Christ he and Paul proclaimed, they both want to make sure that the first Christians at Corinth and elsewhere in Asia Minor are aware of the dangers, and that their faith is firmly grounded in the only true Christ. It is also easy to forget that what Peter said about Jesus is just as important for twenty-first-century Christians as it was for those who lived in the first century – perhaps even more so, as we shall see as this chapter unfolds.

Jesus in Peter's epistles

One only has to read through Peter's epistles, especially 1 Peter, to see how frequently he refers to Jesus. Those who first read these letters would have been in no doubt that Christ was at the very heart of the faith they had so recently espoused, and that everything else Peter wrote was to be seen in this light. First Peter begins by referring to Jesus as the One whom Peter follows, and 2 Peter ends with an exhortation to 'grow in the grace and knowledge of our Lord and Savior Jesus Christ'. In the eight chapters between these two texts Peter refers directly to Jesus fifty-three times, either by name or by using the personal pronouns 'He', 'Him' and 'His'. The scope of what he says about Christ in these chapters is quite remarkable, and it is woven into the text in a way that constantly brings us back to the Person of Jesus and to what is essential to know about Him and the salvation He offers. If Peter's first readers believed and practised what he told them, they would have been Christians without knowing it. Christ and His salvation are like a scarlet thread running through Peter's letters from beginning to end.

Peter refers to the Person of Jesus or to His involvement in the plan of salvation in every chapter of his epistles, but not in a progressive or theological sequence, as might be expressed today in a more structured treatise. Rather, Peter mentions them at points where he feels they might be of help to his readers, as we would expect of letters written from pastoral concern for the spiritual welfare of his people. These essentials concerning Christ are listed below in a more chronological or theological sequence intended to convey the fullness of what he says about who Jesus was and what He accomplished:

- The necessity of a knowledge of Christ (2 Peter 1:8; 2:20)
- His coming, determined before Creation (1 Peter 1:20)
- The divinity of Christ (2 Peter 1:1-3)
- The sinlessness of Christ (1 Peter 1:19)
- His suffering and shed blood (1 Peter 1:11, 19; 4:13)
- His substitutionary death on the cross (1 Peter 2:24)
- His resurrection (1 Peter 3:21)
- His priestly ministry in heaven (1 Peter 3:22)
- Jesus as the source of salvation (1 Peter 1:3-5, 18, 19)
- Christ's righteousness, which enables those 'in Him' to be blameless (1 Peter 2:21-24; 2 Peter 3:14)
- The lordship of Christ, in the Church and in the believer (1 Peter 1:3; 2 Peter 2:1)
- His soon return to complete the work of salvation (1 Peter 5:4; 2 Peter 3:12-14)

Interspersed with these assertions, all of them crucial to a full understanding of who Jesus was and what He has done and will do, are words like 'faith', 'grace', 'peace', 'love' and 'hope' – some of which are mentioned only once, and others of which occur many times, but all of which are helpful in describing the scope of the Gospel and the faith of those who have accepted who Christ is and what He has accomplished.

Peter's most frequently used title for Jesus is 'Lord Jesus Christ', reminding believers of the lordship of Christ as the One who is worthy of worship and worthy to be followed. Peter himself appears to have been convinced of that, as he begins both epistles by stating that he is an 'apostle' of Jesus Christ. The repeated emphasis on the sufferings of Christ, notably in 1 Peter, may be an intentional reminder that, in the trials and persecution they will soon be called to endure, they will be able to identify with Him, their 'Saviour', 'Shepherd' and 'Lord', knowing that He has been there before and knows what it means to suffer.

The cross
The cross is the universally recognised symbol of the Christian Church and of Christianity itself. It represents the crucifixion of Christ and therefore His death. It is well to remember that there is no redemptive power in the symbol, only in what it represents: Christ's death. Peter is recorded in the book of Acts as the first Christian preacher, repeatedly proclaiming the reality of the recent death of Christ in the first days of nascent Christianity, and fearlessly laying the blame on the Jewish leaders. Preaching in the temple forecourt, he charged them of denying 'the Holy One' and of killing 'the Prince of life'. Addressing the Sanhedrin, the 'rulers of the people and elders of Israel', he spoke to them of Christ, 'whom you crucified' (Acts 2:22-24; 3:13-15; 4:8-10). Peter must be credited with shaping the Christ-centred beliefs and witness of the early church, and thereby of the entire Church throughout history. Barclay says of Acts 2 that it records 'the first Christian sermon ever preached', and that it is a 'plain proclamation of the facts of the Christian Gospel', foremost of which are the crucifixion and the resurrection of Christ.

The first chapter of John Stott's acclaimed book *The Cross of Christ* is entitled 'The Centrality of the Cross'. After a comprehensive and lucid account of the continuing importance of the cross, he concludes the chapter by quoting an Anglican scholar, Stephen Neil, who wrote:

> 'In the Christian theology of history, the death of Christ is the central point of history; here all the roads of the past converge; here all the roads to the future diverge.'

It has been said of the crucifixion itself that it was both 'the high point of the Gospel and its lowest level of abject humiliation and suffering'. Harry Lowe, in his book *Redeeming Grace*, describes the cross as 'the focal point of redeeming grace', reminding us that the four gospels give approximately a quarter of their total length to the last week of Christ's life, culminating in His death on Calvary.

It is not surprising, then, that Peter refers to the death of Christ in every chapter of the first epistle. Yet he does so without once mentioning the word 'cross'. It is worth noting in passing that the cross itself was rarely used as a symbol of the Christian faith before the fourth century, long after Constantine had declared Christianity an official religion of the Roman Empire, c. AD 320 (the exact date is still debated). Referring to 1 Peter 2:21-24 and 3:18, Stott says that Peter gave 'profound instruction about the Saviour's death', pointing out that Christ's death was a fulfilment of the Messianic prophecy of Isaiah 53. Stott refers to Peter's epistles or quotes them directly more than fifty times in *The Cross of Christ,* the most frequently quoted texts being 1 Peter 2:24 and 3:18. Grudem says that the former is 'the heart of the Gospel' and that Christ is set forth here 'as a substitute for His people, One who stood in their place'.

The death of Christ is the central point of history; here all the roads of the past converge.

The significance of Christ's death on the cross can be summarised in four words – 'sacrifice', 'suffering', 'substitution' and 'salvation' – all concepts which were understood and alluded to by Peter. Yet surely he would have been the first to say that he had not explored any of them in the depth they deserved. He would probably have agreed that even the witness of the New Testament as a whole did not say all that could be said. Since then, thousands of books have been written about the cross, the crucifixion and the death of Christ. There are six in front of me as I write, and their titles alone are sufficient to demonstrate the centrality of the cross in Christian thinking and its significance as the enduring symbol of Christianity:

- *The Apostolic Preaching of the Cross*
- *The Cross of Christ*
- *The Cross in The New Testament*
- *The Cross and its Shadow*
- *The Empty Cross of Jesus*
- *The Meaning of the Cross*

Yet for all these, and the countless other books which have been written about the cross and the crucifixion, the full meaning of the cross and the depth of Christ's condescension still defy exhaustive explanation.

> 'He suffered the death which was ours, that we might receive the life that was His.'

Stott summarises the significance of Christ's death by saying simply that 'Christ died for our sins', pointing out that this simple affirmation implies much more than it appears to do on the surface. 'It affirms that Jesus Christ – who, being sinless, had no need to die – died our death, the death our sins deserved.' These words are reminiscent of the much-quoted statement by Ellen White in *The Desire of Ages*:

> 'Christ was treated as we deserve, that we might be treated as He deserved. He was condemned for our sins, in which He had no share, that we might be justified by His righteousness, in which we had no share. He suffered the death which was ours, that we might receive the life that was His.'

There is so much more that could be said, but Peter summarised it well when he wrote: 'Christ also suffered for us ... who Himself bore our sins in His own body on the tree, that we ... might live' (1 Peter 2:21, 24).

The shepherd analogy

Peter refers to Jesus as the 'Shepherd and Overseer' of His people (1 Peter 2:25). The word 'shepherd' is derived from the Old English *sceaphirde*, from which we get the words 'sheep' and 'herd': literally, one who herds sheep. A shepherd can only exist if there are sheep. Further, the word can only be fully understood if the nature of sheep is first understood. They are prone to wander aimlessly, and will readily follow one which has assumed the role of leader and taken off without any apparent sense of direction or destination. Peter says that this was once the condition of those to whom he was writing: 'You were like sheep going astray,' but the Shepherd saw your plight, and brought you back to the fold. It is another perspective of Jesus and His task of bringing salvation to a lost world.

Christian People

Many of these early Christians came from a Jewish background. The twelve disciples were all Jewish, and at first Christianity was widely regarded to be a Jewish sect. They would have been familiar with Old Testament references to sheep and shepherds – notably, perhaps, Psalm 23; Isaiah 53:6; and Ezekiel 34:23 – all in some way prophetic of Jesus, portraying Him as He would later portray Himself: 'The Good Shepherd'. Psalm 23 describes a shepherd who cares for the sheep and guides the flock, leading them to feed safely in green pastures and to drink freely from still waters, protected from sheep thieves and the attacks of wild animals. The shepherd in Bible times led the flock; he knew them by name; and when they heard his voice, they willingly followed. Clowney says about Jesus:

> 'He looked with compassion on the scattered sheep of Israel and gathered the remnant flock, calling His own sheep by name. He promised also to gather other sheep: the scattered flock of the Gentiles. They, too, were "like sheep going astray" but have now been brought back by the Shepherd.'

'You meet him, sleepless, far-sighted, weather-beaten, armed, leaning on his staff, and looking out over his scattered sheep, every one of them on his heart.'

The prominent Scottish Old Testament scholar, George Adam Smith, describes in his *Historical Geography of the Holy Land* his own recollections of travelling in Palestine. There are few better descriptions of Judean shepherds:

> 'I do not ever remember to have seen in the East a flock of sheep without a shepherd. In such a landscape as Judea . . . the man and his character are inseparable. On some high moor, across which at night the hyenas howl, when you meet him, sleepless, far-sighted, weather-beaten, armed, leaning on his staff, and looking out over his scattered sheep, every one of them on his heart, you understand why the shepherd of Judea sprang to the front in his people's history; why they gave his name to their king; and why Christ took him as the type of self-sacrifice.'

When Jesus called Himself 'The Good Shepherd' it implies that not all shepherds were good. Some were hirelings, careless and unconcerned, or intent on peddling heresy, as Peter makes clear in his second epistle: 'wolves' in 'sheep's clothing', as Jesus illustrates in Matthew 7:15. Jesus, by contrast, was the epitome and fulfilment of the faithful Judean shepherd. It is yet another dimension of what it means to be Christian and to live as End Time people – faithful followers of the Good Shepherd, and willing to be and to go where He leads.

> Shepherds have no significance whatever unless there are sheep. It is the sheep that really matter.

In his commentary Clowney devotes several pages to dealing with Peter's use of the terms 'shepherd' and 'chief shepherd', showing the importance of shepherds and their sheep in Peter's thinking. Commenting on 1 Peter 2:24, he further writes:

'Christ's atoning sacrifice has accomplished our salvation. We were like sheep going astray, but now we have been brought back to the Shepherd and Overseer of our souls. Jesus is not only the Good Shepherd, who gives His life for the sheep; He is also the Seeking Shepherd, the Lord who gathers His remnant flock.'

These words reflect the thinking of more than one biblical scholar, many of whom have spent much time attempting to understand Peter's letters and their continuing significance to Christians today. The essential point in all this is that shepherds have no significance whatever unless there are sheep. It is the sheep that really matter. In the same way, the cross has no significance without sinners. The cross would never have been associated with Christianity had it not been for sin and sinners. To quote Clowney again:

'Peter says that he is a witness of Christ's sufferings and one who will also share in the glory to be revealed. He witnessed to the sufferings of Christ he had seen in Gethsemane and on Calvary; he witnessed to the glory of Christ he had seen on the Mount of Transfiguration and after the resurrection. . . . Peter's words remind us of Paul's charge to the elders of Ephesus. Paul reminds them that he has borne witness to the Gospel to Jews and Greeks (Gentiles), enduring trials and plots against his life. He pleads with the elders to remember his example, and to shepherd the flock, the Church of God, purchased with His blood.'

We are forever indebted to Peter for bringing to the attention of those first Christians, and to our attention, the deep meaning of Jesus as Shepherd and His concern for the sheep, and for reminding us of the cross and the sacrificial and substitutionary death of Christ on Calvary.

It is unnecessary to quote much more from those who through the centuries have written about the cross and the crucifixion, although to do so would enrich our own perception and understanding. We will, therefore, note just two more comments in closing this brief account of that momentous event in history, which Peter himself witnessed and to which he bore testimony. Frank Colquhoun describes the cross as the key to the 'deepest mysteries concerning God and the world, man and sin, life and death', and says:

> 'The mystery is twofold. The Gospel stresses the fact that Christ died; but it is perfectly clear from what the Bible tells us on the one hand that He *need* not have died, and on the other hand that He *ought* not to have died.'

James Atkinson says that the preaching of the cross in the early days of Christianity, and this we have already noted, was largely due to Peter's sermons on and after the Day of Pentecost, which 'fired the imagination and stirred the will of the ancient world'. He then explains:

> 'The cross was the only way through an impasse created when the righteous God meets unrighteous man, who, in his wilful disobedience to the revealed, righteous will of God, earns the curse and hostility of God. This same God in Christ faced the full fury of sin and unbelief in its onslaught to destroy Him. Though righteous and innocent, He took the punishment for sin and unbelief and was treated as the worst sinner. He defeated sin by

Though righteous and innocent, He took the punishment for sin and unbelief.

never succumbing to it, and thereby overcame death and mortality. As the willing victim, He destroyed the curse by taking it on Himself, thereby defeating a hitherto invincible power, and in breaking this power He released men from its bondage and tyranny into a new and eternal freedom.'

All this is what it meant to Peter's readers to be human and Christian in a foreign land and a hostile world, as indeed it does to their spiritual descendants today.

There is an old gospel song made famous by George Beverly Shea and heard by millions around the world during the Billy Graham crusades of the 1950s and '60s. Based on Jesus' parable of the lost sheep, and perhaps on Christ's words to Peter after the resurrection, 'Feed My lambs and sheep,' as recorded in John 21, it is a skilful blend of the biblical story and the poetic insight of a newly converted young Christian, Elizabeth Clephane, from Melrose in Scotland. She would have known well the majestic Scottish Highlands, home to more sheep than people. I can still hear Beverly Shea's rich baritone voice even now as I type these words:

> 'Though the road may be rough and steep, I go to the desert to find My sheep.'

There were ninety and nine that safely lay
in the shelter of the fold,
But one was out on the hills away,
far off from the streets of gold –
Away on the mountains wild and bare,
away from the tender Shepherd's care.

'Lord, Thou hast here Thy ninety and nine;
are they not enough for Thee?'
But the Shepherd made answer:
'This of Mine has wandered away from Me,
And though the road may be rough and steep,
I go to the desert to find My sheep.'

*But none of the ransomed ever knew
how deep were the waters crossed;
Nor how dark the night the Lord passed through
'ere He found the sheep that was lost.
Out in the desert He heard its cry,
sick and helpless and ready to die.*

*But all through the mountains, thunder-riven,
and up from the rocky steep
There arose a glad cry to the gate of heaven,
'Rejoice! I have found My sheep!'
And the angels echoed around the throne,
'Rejoice, for the Lord brings back His own.'*

For reflection and further study

Take another look at the quotation from *The Desire of Ages* by Ellen White on page 36. How do these few lines and 1 Peter 2:21, 24 help us understand the meaning and heart of the Gospel?

4 People of the Word

When Christians speak of the Word of God they generally mean one of two things – the written word, the Scriptures of the Old and New Testaments; or the incarnate Word, God Himself in the human form of Jesus. While Jesus is unquestionably the ultimate revelation of God to humankind, the two are closely and inseparably connected. Apart from four or five incidental references to the existence of Jesus in Jewish and Roman histories, all that is known about Him from original sources comes directly from the Bible. More books have been written about Jesus than any other person in history – many of them enlightening and perceptive, but none of them having the status of God's inspired word, the Holy Scriptures. W. Graham Scroggie, writing in R. T. Kendall's *The Word of the Lord*, reminds us:

> 'The Bible which makes the redeeming God known to us is our most precious heritage.'

> 'Christians do not worship the Bible, but the God who is revealed in it; but we do realise, or we ought to, that the Bible which makes the redeeming God known to us is our most precious heritage.'

When Peter first refers to the word of God, he declares that it has three fundamental characteristics. It is the word which is alive, the word which transforms, and the word which is eternal. Speaking of the experience of recently converted readers, he says they have been 'born again, not of corruptible seed but incorruptible, through the word of God which lives and abides forever' (1 Peter 1:23). These truths have profound implications which would take us far beyond the limitations of this chapter were we to explore them. In *The Vocabulary of the Bible* there is a well-informed entry about the Word of God, in which the author emphasises the crucial importance of the Word in the relationship between God and humanity, saying, 'It is the essential mode whereby God intervenes in the world. . . . The whole history of salvation to which Scripture is the witness is the word which God addresses to the world.' He goes on to say that it is 'dynamic', 'creative' and 'prophetic', and that in God's own time and redemptive purpose this word was 'made flesh'. All this is fundamental to everything Peter says about the word in his epistles – which, as we shall see, is considerable.

The Old Testament Scriptures
Peter uses the word 'Scripture' three times: in 1 Peter 2:6; 2 Peter 1:20; and 3:16. The English word is derived from the Latin *scriptura*, meaning 'writing' or 'something written', and in the New Testament it is always translated from the Greek *graphe*, also meaning 'writing'. The related English word 'graphic' means 'giving clear and vividly explicit details'. That is precisely what the Old Testament Scriptures are: a collection of thirty-nine books, the writings of historians and prophets who faithfully recorded what they had seen, heard or been told.

When Peter speaks of Scripture, however, he does not mean what is meant by the word today. He means only the collected books of the Old Testament as they were known in his day, whereas today Scripture refers to the whole Bible, including the New Testament – much of which, including all the books written by John and some of Paul's later epistles, was still unwritten when Peter wrote his letters (c. AD 64/65). He frequently cites the Old Testament as a source of authoritative truth.

Peter's knowledge and use of the Old Testament text is remarkable. He refers to it by direct quotation or through allusion in every chapter of his epistles. In 1 Peter there are thirteen quotations from the Old Testament and eight specific allusions to Old Testament people, places or events. The most quoted books are Isaiah and Psalms, but he also quotes from Exodus, Leviticus, Proverbs and Ezekiel. The allusions include Abraham and Sarah, Noah and the Ark, and God's people, Israel. In 2 Peter the pattern is much the same. Quotations are taken from Daniel and Proverbs, and the allusions include the Genesis Creation record, Noah and the Flood, Sodom and Gomorrah, Lot, and Balaam and his donkey. The phrase in 2 Peter 3:12 which describes the melting of the earth in the fires of the last day is a direct reference to Micah 1:4, 'The mountains will melt under Him.'

Peter weaves all this and more into his epistles to explain or illustrate what he wants to say, and in a way that it becomes an integral part of the text, flowing freely and clearly. A notable example is 2 Peter 3:9: 'The Lord is not slack concerning His promise, as some count slackness, but is longsuffering toward us, not willing that any should perish but that all should come to repentance.' Unless it was pointed out, most readers would be unaware that there are in this text allusions to Habakkuk, Isaiah and Ezekiel, all brought together to make a clear and affirming statement about the purposes of God and the merciful provisions of His grace.

Particularly notable in this respect is the extent to which Peter finds Christ in the Old Testament, especially in Isaiah, the 'Gospel prophet'. Peter mentions the name of Christ more than fifty times in his epistles, making Christ relevant to his readers by reminding them not only of Christ's sufferings and substitutionary death, as foretold in Isaiah 53, but also of His resurrection, priestly ministry and second coming. The first-century End Time people would have been greatly encouraged and established in their faith when they read Peter's epistles and understood the truth and reliability of the Old Testament

Scriptures and their testimony to the One they had chosen to follow. Wayne Grudem concludes that Peter's use of the Old Testament indicates that in the mind of his readers what the Old Testament said was 'able to be trusted completely'.

Commenting on 1 Peter 1:12, R. C. H. Lenski, a meticulous Greek scholar, remarks on the close relationship between the Old and New Testaments in their witness to the Gospel. Having previously commented on the quest of the prophets to enquire about the salvation available in Christ, and yet to be finally revealed (1 Peter 1:5-12), Lenski declares:

> 'The whole New Testament Gospel rests on the Spirit's Old Testament testimony that was made through the Old Testament prophets. Cancel that testimony, and you remove the basis of the Gospel of Christ. It was revealed to the prophets that their ministry was to be far wider than a ministry merely for themselves and for their time; it was a ministry for all the future ages, for Peter's readers as well as for us to this day.'

Particularly notable in this respect is the extent to which Peter finds Christ in the Old Testament, especially in Isaiah, the 'Gospel prophet'.

Some years ago, I came across the record of an elderly lady who lived in seventeenth-century England, a time when strange religious views and eccentric people were not uncommon. She belonged to a little non-conformist church known for its strict adherence to the Scriptures, and became so enamoured with the Old Testament that she tore the entire New Testament from her Bible. Clearly she had a point to make, but one feels that a reaction like that might have been just a bit over the top! Apart from this misguided lady, authentic End Time people of every age and from many nations would forever be grateful to Peter for emphasising that the Old Testament Scriptures were the word of God, and for demonstrating their continuing relevance.

The prophetic word

Second Peter 1:16-21 is one of the key passages in the entire Bible regarding the word of God. Its basic message is the trustworthiness of the prophetic word and the conclusions which inevitably arise from that fact. This passage must be seen in the immediate context of Peter's personal witness to Christ's appearance on the Mount of Transfiguration (see Matthew 17:1-5). Peter was there. He saw and heard what took place. This account has all the hallmarks of personal testimony.

So in verse 18 he is in effect saying, 'You'd better listen to this and believe it, because I know what I'm talking about.'

> Peter was there. He saw and heard what took place. This account has all the hallmarks of personal testimony.

There is, however, something more fundamental here. The prophetic word of Scripture is even more certain than Peter's personal witness to the Transfiguration. The marginal reading of verse 19 in the NKJV is, 'We also have the more sure prophetic word.' The 1984 edition of the NIV says that the word of the prophets has been 'made more certain' by the events of the Transfiguration, particularly by the voice of God affirming His Son, which Peter saw with his own eyes and heard with his own ears. Barclay goes a step further when he paraphrases the essential message of verses 18 and 19: 'What he saw on the Mount of Transfiguration makes it even more certain that what is foretold in the prophets about the Second Coming must be true.'

Peter then emphasises the inescapable consequence of the trustworthiness of the prophetic word. 'You do well to heed' it, he says; or, as the NIV puts it, 'You will do well to pay attention to it . . . until the day dawns.' Why? Because it is like a lamp in a dark place in which the darkness will grow even darker until the coming of Christ. Michael Green comments on this passage in some detail, and concludes:

> 'Whatever the precise details, the main emphasis is manifest: we are on pilgrimage throughout our lives in this dark world. God has graciously provided us with a lamp, the Scriptures. If we pay attention to them for reproof, warning, guidance and encouragement, we shall walk safely. If we neglect them, we shall be engulfed by darkness.'

Verse 21 provides a further reason for paying attention to God's prophetic word – its divine origin. 'For prophecy never came by the will of man, but holy men of God spoke as they were moved by the Holy Spirit.' Green says of this text that it is 'perhaps the fullest and most explicit biblical reference to the inspiration of its authors'. Without going into the details of the doctrine of inspiration, we can say with confidence that the authority of the prophetic word is that it is God's word. The prophets were God's chosen spokesmen. Again, the marginal alternative to the phrase in verse 20, 'private interpretation', is 'private origin'. There is clearly a difference between interpretation and origin. Peter's preference for the marginal translation 'origin' seems confirmed when he states, 'For prophecy never had its origin in the human will, but prophets, though human, spoke from God as they were carried along by the Holy Spirit' (verse 21, NIV). It is impossible to avoid the conclusion that if the prophets were God's inspired spokesmen then their words carried divine authority.

It should be noted that all this refers equally to prophecy in either of its two meanings – predictive prophecy, probably the meaning that usually comes to mind first when the word 'prophecy' is mentioned, or prophecy which is proclaimed when the prophet faithfully declares the word of God, whether it relates to the future or the present. The bottom line is that all prophetic words are God's words, trustworthy and authoritative. Citing again the *Vocabulary of the Bible:*

'Prophecy, then, is not simple prediction: it is a proclamation of God's intentions with regard to His people and the world; it is a message spoken before somebody just as much as before such-and-such an event.'

The word of truth

The words of Jesus inevitably come to mind when considering truth. In His intercessory prayer to the Father, recorded in John 17, He declares: 'Thy word is truth' (verse 17, KJV), praying that His Father will 'sanctify' the disciples or 'set them apart' through the truth. Truth is here presented not only as a concept to be understood, but also as a living, enabling, ennobling power, active in Christian thought and conduct. Although Peter did not write these words, we can be sure that

> Prophecy, then, is not simple prediction: it is a proclamation of God's intentions.

he would have agreed with them readily. In fact, as we shall see, he wrote in a similar vein in 2 Peter 1:5-15. In Kendall's book, *The Word of the Lord*, Crossley Morgan evaluates the truth claims of the Bible in the light of Christ's teaching that a good tree cannot bring forth bad fruit (Matthew 7:18).

'If the book is not true when it claims to speak with the authority of heaven itself, then you have an impossible thing happening down through the centuries of history. If this book is not true when it claims to be the word of God, then you have a book saturated with a lie from cover to cover bringing forth good fruit wherever it goes. That is impossible.'

The concept of truth – reality, accuracy, factuality – has been fundamental to Christianity from the beginning. So, when Peter writes about truth, he knows that his readers will know what he means. He says, 'I will not be negligent to remind you always of these things, though you know and are established in the present truth' (2 Peter 1:12). He reminds them not only that they 'know' the truth and have been 'established' in it, but also that they will 'always have a reminder of these things' after his decease (verse 15). This text has significant implications for us, as it did for them, and to grasp its full meaning it must also be read in context, as has been said previously of other texts.

'These things' are laid out in some detail in the preceding passage, verses 5-11, which mention, among other things, that these early Christian believers have a knowledge of Jesus Christ (verse 8); that they have been cleansed from sin (verse 9); that they have been called to godly living (verses 5-7); and that they have been promised certain entrance into the coming kingdom of Christ (verse 11). 'These things' are the basic facts of Christian belief and conduct, the 'truth' they have come to know. These are the truths they have known from the beginning and in which they have been established. Michael Green says of this passage, 'Truth will bear repetition,' adding that when Peter wrote these words he was fulfilling one of the prime duties of a Christian leader: namely, to 'keep the basic facts of Christian truth and conduct always before the minds of his congregation' – in Peter's case, the new believers in the recently established churches in Asia Minor. The same, of course, applies today. Truth will always bear repetition.

There is, however, a difficulty with Peter's reference to 'present truth'. It has at times been taken to mean that truth is progressive; that what once was true is no longer true. In some realms of human thought and endeavour this is undoubtedly the case. That which was once considered true in physics, medicine and astronomy, for example, is now considered obsolete. New knowledge has come to light; truth has developed and advanced. But this is not the case with the truths of Christianity as revealed in the Scriptures. Our perceptions of truth can change as we grow in grace and in the knowledge of Jesus, as Peter admonishes at the end of his second epistle. But it is unthinkable that He who declared Himself to be 'the Way, the Truth, and the Life' could or would withdraw these claims as no longer credible. While perceptions of truth can change, revealed truth itself is absolute.

So what does Peter mean when he speaks of 'present' truth? Other translations of this text help us here. For 'present truth', the NIV says, 'the truth you now have'. In other words, there was a time when Peter's readers didn't have it. The NLT reads, 'the truth you have been taught', implying that there was a time when they were ignorant of the truth. And the GNB, referring to the context of this verse, the basics of Christian faith, says, 'even though you already know them and are firmly grounded in the truth you have received'. They may have needed reminding of the things they had come to know and understand when they first believed, but the truth itself was still the same.

David Wells, a distinguished professor of biblical theology and much-read author, writes about the truth as first understood by the apostles and early Christians and later set forth in the New Testament. Referring to Peter's epistles and other New Testament writers, he says that the apostolic world was a cauldron of conflicting claims:

'. . . within which the Christian movement would have

remained tiny but for one fact: the first Christians knew that their faith was absolutely true. . . . Why were they so adamant about the preservation and propagation of this teaching? The answer is that it is the *truth* [several New Testament references are cited here, including 1 Peter 1:22; 2 Peter 1:12]. The whole apostolic message about God, His character, His acts, especially as they were revealed in Christ, became the substance of their faith, the foundation without which one cannot have Christian faith.'

> This stark warning to End Time people in the first century is also relevant to End Time people living in the last of the last days – perhaps, indeed, even more timely.

The decline of truth

Peter's other references to truth are more alarming. Having stated that there are those who are 'disobedient to the word' (1 Peter 2:8), he later explains how this has happened, and says that it will get worse. Beginning with the fact that 'false prophets' existed in Old Testament times, he says, 'There will be false teachers among you,' and 'many will follow their destructive ways, because of whom the way of truth will be blasphemed' (2 Peter 2:1, 2) – or, as the NIV puts it, 'Many will follow their depraved conduct and will bring the way of truth into disrepute.' In view of other New Testament statements about the rise of false teaching in the infant church (for example, Acts 20:29, 30), we should not be surprised that all this was happening within a generation of the death and resurrection of Christ. Of more significance, this stark warning to End Time people in the first century is also relevant to End Time people living in the last of the last days – perhaps, indeed, even more timely.

Space once again prevents us from pursuing this sobering theme as much as it deserves, but Dr David Wells' book, *No Place for Truth: Or Whatever Happened to Evangelical Theology?* is a serious and timely comment on the status of truth in this End Time. In one of the most articulate and comprehensive critiques of evangelical Christianity at the end of the twentieth century, Wells exposes the departure from biblical truth in the evangelical world. We may well feel that what Dr Wells says is even more relevant now in the twenty-first century:

> 'I have watched with growing disbelief as the evangelical Church has cheerfully plunged into astounding theological illiteracy.... The effects of this great change in the evangelical soul are evident in every incoming class in the seminaries, in most publications, in the great majority of churches, and in most of their pastors.... We now have less biblical fidelity, less interest in truth, less seriousness, less depth, and less capacity to speak to our own generation.... The new evangelicalism is not driven by the same passion for truth.'

The similarities between Peter's day and ours are obvious – disobedience to the word of truth, false teachers and destructive heresies.

> 'What has changed is that now the whole of society has become avant-garde.... Society is now engaged in this massive experiment to do what no other major civilisation has done – to rebuild itself deliberately and self-consciously without religious foundations.... Truth in any absolute sense has gone.'

Dr Wells goes on to outline the effects of all this in the Church, in the world, and in the lives of individual believers. It is little short of a catalogue of disaster for all concerned:

> 'Biblical interest in righteousness is replaced by a search for happiness, holiness by wholeness, truth by feeling, ethics by feeling good about oneself. The world shrinks to the range of personal circumstances; the community of faith shrinks to a circle of friends. The past recedes. The Church recedes. The world recedes. All that remains is the self.... The heretics of old, one suspects, would be sick with envy if they knew of the easy pickings that can now be had in the Church.'

The similarities between Peter's day and ours are obvious – disobedience to the word of truth, false teachers and destructive heresies, on account of which the way of truth has been brought into disrepute. But there is a significant difference. It is the extent and the depth of the heresy now

The light has shone in the darkness, and the darkness has not and will not extinguish it. peddled, the strength of the opposition from within as well as from without, and the deepening effect on the surrounding culture, all of which are much greater today than in Peter's day. The sheer scale of the antipathy, not only in North America, but elsewhere across the English-speaking world, could not have been imagined even in the mid-twentieth century.

While all this is true and probably irreversible, we should not allow these sobering realities to detract from all that Peter has said about the Old Testament Scriptures, the prophetic word and the word of truth. They are also realities for End Time people living at the very end of time. The light has shone in the darkness, and the darkness has not and will not extinguish it. In the last verse of his much-loved hymn, 'Once to Every Man and Nation', written in 1845, James Russell Lowell recognised such a reality, but sang of hope. On this positive note we will conclude our survey of Peter's message about God's unchanging word in a changing world:

> *Though the cause of evil prosper,*
> *Yet the truth alone is strong;*
> *Though her portion be the scaffold,*
> *And upon the throne be wrong;*
> *Yet that scaffold sways the future,*
> *And behind the dim unknown*
> *Standeth God within the shadow,*
> *Keeping watch above His own.*

For reflection and further study

1. 'Thy Word is truth,' says Jesus in John 17; and, as chapter 4 points out, 'The concept of truth, reality, accuracy and factuality has been fundamental to Christianity from the beginning.'
2. In an era when 'truth in any absolute sense has gone', what are the challenges, and what are the opportunities, as to how we share the Gospel?

Spirit-led People 5

At the end of his sermon on the Day of Pentecost, Peter made a prophetic promise of profound significance and far-reaching implications for individual believers, as well as for the Christian Church itself:

'Then Peter said to them, "Repent, and let every one of you be baptized in the name of Jesus Christ for the remission of sins; and you shall receive the gift of the Holy Spirit. For the promise is to you and to your children, *and to all who are afar off, as many as the Lord our God will call*" ' (Acts 2:38, 39, emphasis supplied).

It is difficult, if not impossible, to overstate how crucial the fulfilment of this promise was to the inauguration of the Christian Church. Speaking of Pentecost, William Barclay points out: 'From that moment the Holy Spirit became the dominant reality in the life of the early church.' Pentecost introduced a new era, not only in the history of the Church, but also in the history of mankind. This was, and still is, the age of the Spirit, for there is no indication in the book of Acts or in any other book of the New Testament that the Spirit returned to heaven after His

> 'Repent, and let every one of you be baptized in the name of Jesus Christ for the remission of sins; and you shall receive the gift of the Holy Spirit.'

descent at Pentecost. All New Testament time is in fact the age of the Spirit, and the promise made on that day was as much for all who came after it had been made as it was for those then living. It is still for us as much as it was for them.

> These things would surely have been imprinted indelibly on Peter's mind, never to be forgotten.

Peter's qualifications

Following the resurrection Peter was recognised as the first leader among the early believers, soon becoming the spokesman for the infant church, as is evident in the early chapters of Acts. He had been one of those first called by Jesus to be a disciple (Mark 1:16, 17). He had heard Jesus speak in great detail about the Holy Spirit, 'the Spirit of truth', a 'Helper' ('Comforter', KJV), who would guide them, glorify Christ, and speak of 'things to come' (John 14:16, 17; 16:13, 14). Peter had also been present on the Day of Pentecost and had witnessed the extraordinary events of that day – the sound of 'a rushing mighty wind' filling the house where the believers were assembled, tongues 'as of fire' descending on the waiting apostles, their ability to speak in other languages 'as the Spirit gave them utterance' (Acts 2:1-4) – the promised outpouring of the Holy Spirit, as had been predicted in the book of Joel (2:28-32; Acts 2:16-21). These things would surely have been imprinted indelibly on Peter's mind, never to be forgotten – perhaps because they had not only been seen and heard by Peter himself and others who were present, but also changed those who were there. As Barclay says, 'The disciples had an experience of the power of the Spirit flooding into their beings such as they never had before.'

The record also states that in those early days of the fledgling Christian movement Peter himself was 'filled with the Holy Spirit', performing miracles: the healing of a lame man and then a paralytic (Acts 3:4-8 and 9:34), and raising Dorcas from her death-bed (Acts 9:39, 40). It is also recorded that, in Jerusalem and neighbouring towns, crowds brought out the sick into the streets, hoping that Peter's shadow might fall on them so that they would be healed (Acts 5:15, 16). In fact, Peter is mentioned by name nearly fifty times in the first few chapters of Acts, on most occasions in association with the Holy Spirit. There were few, if any, better qualified to speak to the early Christians about the Holy Spirit than Peter.

The Holy Spirit in the book of Acts
It has been said that the book of Acts might better have been called 'The Acts of the Holy Spirit' rather than 'The Acts of the Apostles'. The truth is that it was both: the Spirit working 'many signs and wonders' through the apostles on an almost daily basis (Acts 5:12). Barclay says that in one respect 'Acts is the most important book in the New Testament,' because without it we would have very little knowledge about the early church – or, what may be more important, no record of the mighty working of the Holy Spirit in those early years.

One only has to read the first few chapters of Acts to be convinced of Peter's stature in the early church. His presence can almost be felt: a figure looming large above all others in those first weeks and months of the Church's existence. He is nearly always there, speaking and acting as the Spirit directed and used him. But the dominant presence in those unprecedented times was that of the Spirit Himself. He is found on every page and in every chapter that tells of the birth and growth of the early church, specifically in Acts chapters 1-12.

Luke, the respected historian of the early Christian church, records in Acts 10:19 that the Holy Spirit spoke directly to Peter about the meaning of a vision he had seen but not understood. So that he might understand, it is recorded that the Spirit told Peter to go with six other believers to a certain house where, when he began to speak, 'the Holy Spirit fell upon them, as upon us at the beginning' (Acts 11:15). The record says that after this incident Peter was accused of eating with Gentiles, and he defended himself by reminding his accusers of the facts – that the Holy Spirit had fallen upon these Gentiles in a visible manner. Barclay notes that Peter had taken six others with him, making seven in all, and points out that in some legal situations

> **But the dominant presence in those unprecedented times was that of the Spirit Himself. He is found on every page.**

of the day seven witnesses were necessary to prove a case. He says, 'So Peter is in effect saying, "I am not arguing with you. I am telling you the facts, and of these facts there are seven witnesses. The case is proved." ' The proof was that the Holy Spirit had brought Gentiles into the faith. The early Christian movement was not only for Jewish believers: it was for all who would believe. It was a proven instance for the credibility of Christianity, as well as an example of the Spirit's working in the early church.

Through the working of the Spirit in those days and months the Church grew rapidly. Many specific instances are recorded in the early chapters of Acts, most of which involved Peter: 'Those who gladly received his word were baptized; and that day about three thousand souls were added to them' (Acts 2:41); 'the number of the disciples multiplied greatly in Jerusalem, and a great many of the priests were obedient to the faith' (Acts 6:7); 'the churches throughout all Judea, Galilee, and Samaria had peace and were edified. And . . . they were multiplied' (Acts 9:31); 'and many believed on the Lord' (Acts 9:42); 'and the hand of the Lord was with them, and a great number believed and turned to the Lord' (Acts 11:21). It is a remarkable sequence of events, all made possible by the presence and power of the Holy Spirit working through Peter, and sometimes through others. Reading these accounts, it is self-evident that there was a very close and dynamic connection between the Holy Spirit and Peter: God and man working together, a partnership which resulted in the origin and early growth of the Christian Church, and which has been the model for church growth and stability ever since.

There is another connection, equally important to understanding the epistles of Peter. It is the link between the book of Acts and Peter's epistles, all written at about the same time. The person who wrote the epistles was the same person who had figured so prominently in the establishment of the Church some thirty years previously. The early chapters of Acts illuminate Peter's epistles and help us to understand what he says about the Holy Spirit. The Spirit is mentioned almost fifty times in the first twelve chapters of Acts, and twice as many times in the first seven chapters of Acts as in the eight chapters of Peter's two epistles put together. The book of Acts is an essential background to understanding the epistles of Peter, particularly concerning the Person and work of the Holy Spirit. In Billy Graham's book *The Holy Spirit,* he comments on Pentecost and its long-term consequences:

'The coming of the Holy Spirit on the day of Pentecost marked a crucial turning point in the history of God's dealings with the human race . . . [and] assures us that the Spirit of God has come to achieve His certain purposes in the world, in the church, and in the individual believer.'

Peter's letters, read in the context of Acts, help us to understand the lasting significance of Pentecost and to see its continuing importance for End Time people today.

The Holy Spirit in Peter's epistles
Peter attests to five major truths concerning the Holy Spirit, the first of them at the very beginning of his letters. Writing to the scattered 'pilgrims' of Asia Minor, he says that they are 'elect according to the foreknowledge of God the Father, in sanctification of the Spirit, for obedience and sprinkling of the blood of Jesus Christ' (1 Peter 1:2). While some things in this text are not clear, as previously noted, it refers specifically to the Father, Jesus and the Spirit, confirming the concept of the Trinity, a Christian belief that has not always been understood, even by some in the Church and even by some today.

'The Spirit of God has come to achieve His certain purposes in the world, in the church, and in the individual believer.'

It is said that Patrick, who established Christianity in Ireland in the fifth century, was once asked to explain the Trinity. Bending down, he picked a shamrock leaf and held it up as an illustration of his answer to the question. Like clover, the shamrock leaf has a stalk with three leaflets at the top, each equal in position and with similar functions in relation to the purpose of the leaf itself. If the leaf represents God, Patrick explained, the leaflets represent the three Persons of the Trinity, all equally God and all existing for the same purpose. That being so, the Holy Spirit is equally part of the Godhead,

> 'It is: "One times one times one equals one."'

fully God, His words and works having the same authority as those of the Father and the Son.

Billy Graham points out in his book *The Holy Spirit,* in a chapter entitled 'Who is the Holy Spirit?' that when Christ referred to the Holy Spirit in John chapters 14 to 16 he spoke of a Person, not an influence, the original Greek always using the masculine pronoun 'He' rather than the neutral pronoun 'it'. Similarly, in the Great Commission recorded in Matthew 28:19, 20, the Greek makes it clear that Jesus was referring to three separate Persons. Graham also comments on the apostolic benediction in 2 Corinthians 13:14, which speaks of 'the grace of the Lord Jesus Christ', 'the love of God' and 'the communion of the Holy Spirit', saying:

> 'This benediction clearly indicates that the Holy Spirit is one with the Father and one with the Son in the Godhead. *It is not: "One plus one plus one equals three." It is: "One times one times one equals one."* The Holy Spirit is one with the Father and the Son. If the Father is God, and Jesus is God, then the Holy Spirit is also God.'

John Stott sees it from another perspective: 'The Holy Spirit has sometimes been called the "executive" of the Godhead, meaning that what the Father and the Son desire to do in the world and in the Church today, they execute through the Holy Spirit.' It is not sufficient to believe in the existence of the Holy Spirit, vital as that unquestionably is. He must also be understood, in His very nature and in the source of His unique power. All this is implicit in Peter's allusion to the Trinity in 1 Peter 1:2, affirming the divine personhood of the Holy Spirit.

There is another truth of even greater significance regarding the Holy Spirit in 1 Peter 1:2. The NKJV phrase 'in sanctification of the Spirit' is translated in the NIV as 'through the sanctifying work of the Spirit', and in Phillips' translation of the New Testament as 'to be made holy by his Spirit'. As

> 'But as He who called you is holy, you also be holy in all your conduct' (1 Peter 1:15).

explained in chapter two, where 1 Peter 1:2 was first considered, the words 'sanctification' and 'sanctify' come from the Greek noun *hagiasmos* and verb *hagiazo*, both with a strong connotation of 'holy' or 'holiness'. Peter, in harmony with other New Testament writers – for example, Paul in 2 Thessalonians 2:13 – says that the Holy Spirit is the Agent through whom sanctification takes place, but he does not say when or how it happens. He does, however, talk about holiness and godly living: 'But as He who called you is holy, you also be holy in all your conduct' (1 Peter 1:15), advice that fits well with the dictionary definition of 'sanctify', 'to set apart, or make holy'. He also 'begs' his readers, 'sojourners and pilgrims' in the world, to 'abstain from fleshly lusts which war against the soul', and to ensure that their conduct is 'honorable among the Gentiles' (1 Peter 2:11, 12). This is, in effect, saying that sanctification is an ongoing process, as opposed to justification, which occurs immediately as soon as a person puts his or her faith in Christ.

That the Holy Spirit works continually within to sanctify those who believe is an essential truth of the Gospel, equally as important as justification. In his book *The Office and Work of the Holy Spirit,* James Buchanan states:

> 'Sanctification is the work of the Spirit, and is to be dated from the time of a sinner's conversion. . . . [It is] the continued work of the Spirit in the progressive and growing sanctification of the believer after he has been born again.'

Michael Green illustrates the same truth from the experience of Paul:

> 'It is the work of the Spirit, then, to make us progressively reflect the character of Christ. . . . The process of Christlikeness is a progressive one; let nobody think he has attained it. Paul himself, after decades of knowing Christ, could still say he had not attained the purpose for which Christ had laid hold of him.'

Referring to 1 Peter 1:2, Wayne Grudem, speaking of the three Persons of the Trinity 'uniting to bring about a common goal', says of the sanctifying work of the Spirit that it is 'the work whereby He gradually works in Christians to free them more and more from remaining in sin and to make them increasingly like Christ in holiness, faith, and love'. It is as important to know that sanctification is a progressive work of the Spirit that lasts for the lifetime of a believer as it is to know that it is a work of the Spirit Himself.

Few have explained the work of the Holy Spirit in the Christian life better than William Barclay:

> 'For the Christian, the Holy Spirit is essential to every part of the Christian life and every step in it. It is the Holy Spirit who awakens within us the first faint longings for God and goodness. It is the Holy Spirit who convicts us of our sin and leads us to the cross, where that sin is forgiven. It is the Holy Spirit who enables us to be freed from the sins which have us in their grip, and to gain the virtues which are the fruit of the Spirit. The beginning, the middle and the end of the Christian life are the work of the Holy Spirit.'

> **'The beginning, the middle and the end of the Christian life are the work of the Holy Spirit.'**

Peter would surely have said 'amen' to that; for, as we have noted again here, as previously in earlier chapters, he often speaks of the need for holiness and godly living.

There are, however, two dangers here that are to be avoided. One is the notion that sanctification leads to perfection, a misunderstanding that has often led to erroneous conclusions, even to shipwreck of the faith in some Christians. One authority explains:

> 'The sanctified are by no means perfect. They are beset by innumerable "infirmities" and are liable to all kinds of mistakes, both of judgement and practice, as long as they live, even though they have the love of God filling their hearts and governing their lives.'

Sanctification is the work of a lifetime ... but it is not our work! It is the work of the Spirit, and of Him alone.

The other danger is misunderstanding a phrase that has been, and still is, used widely in some Christian circles, namely that 'sanctification is the work of a lifetime'. Thousands have been misled here, thinking that they must strive day after day and week after week, for the rest of their lives, to be like Christ and to attain holiness. Many have become discouraged, some even giving up and falling away. It is true, as we have seen, that sanctification is the work of a lifetime ... but it is not our work! It is the work of the Spirit, and of Him alone. Speaking of the infilling of the Spirit, Billy Graham says:

> 'When we are filled with the Spirit, it is not a question of there being more of Him, as though His work in us is quantitative. It is not how much of the Spirit we have, but how much He has of us.'

It should never be forgotten that when the Spirit came to the waiting church at Pentecost, He came to stay. We should not be waiting for Him to come again or to come more fully, but rather be open to receive Him because He is already here, waiting for the Church to respond. Graham declares, 'We are no longer waiting for the Holy Spirit – He is waiting for us.'

Finally, a further word about obedience. Peter writes to the early believers, acknowledging that they obey the truth 'through the Spirit' (1 Peter 1:22). Most modern translations omit this phrase because it is not found in many early Greek manuscripts. Although this may be the case, Peter goes on to remind them in verse 23 that they have been born again, an experience that is unarguably the result of the Spirit's work within. Although this is stated in the next verse, verses 22 and 23 are in fact all one sentence. It is not unreasonable to conclude that obedience is brought about as much by the Spirit within as is the new birth. However this may be, Peter affirms that obedience is a consequence of the Spirit's working, enabling obedience and sanctification, characteristics of all authentic End Time believers (cf. 1 Peter 1:2).

Much more might be said, and indeed has been said, and those wishing to pursue this vital topic in depth might well read James Buchanan's *The Office and Work of the Holy Spirit* and/or Billy Graham's *The Holy Spirit*, the latter recommended by John Stott in *Christian Basics*. My own little book, *Living in the Spirit*, was intended to be a practical guide to the work of the Spirit in the lives of End Time people living today.

Sanctification, obedience, holiness, and continuing growth in grace, according to Peter, are all essential characteristics of the Christian life; and all are the special work of the Holy Spirit, the third Person of the Holy Trinity, God Himself working tirelessly for the salvation of the lost. Without Him, the Holy Spirit, we could not be reborn, sanctified, enabled to obey, or saved. James Buchanan says, 'Not only the commencement, but also the continuance of the spiritual life, depends on the gracious operation of the Spirit of God.' One of the most important things that Peter says about the Spirit in his epistles is that He enables believers to be sanctified – set apart and made holy, waiting for the End Time to reach its climactic conclusion when the salvation 'ready to be revealed' at the last day becomes a reality.

I once heard Michael Green preach in the university church in Oxford. It was a memorable experience, and I have respected him as a true evangelical Christian ever since. I have found his book *I Believe in the Holy Spirit,* the first volume in the '*I Believe'* series, helpful more than once since I first read it while teaching at Newbold College of Higher Education. It is the kind of book not easily forgotten. Green says in the chapter on the work of the Spirit in the individual:

'The Holy Spirit is God's gift to us, and God means us not just to read about Him, but . . . to know that we are in Christ, and He has given us the Spirit to assure us. God means us to grow in Christlikeness, and has given us the Spirit to change us. God means to free us from the bondage of the self-centredness and self-vindication which marked us in the old days, and has equipped us with the Spirit of the Messiah to set us free to serve Him unselfconsciously, effectively and joyfully.'

We didn't use our hymn books during the pandemic – more's the pity – but if we had, we might have found the lovely hymn 'Our Blest Redeemer, Ere He Breathed' by Harriet Auber, which contains these words about the Spirit, words it would not be amiss to memorise:

Spirit-led People

And every virtue we possess,
And every victory won,
And every thought of holiness
Are His, and His alone.

Peter may not have had a hymn book like we do, but he did have a personal knowledge and a profound experience of the Spirit's mighty power, which through his writing he commended to all End Time people.

For reflection and further study

'But go, tell His disciples – and Peter . . .' (Mark 16:7). The messenger in the tomb announces, 'He is not here' and insists that the recent denier of Christ – Peter – be informed. How do you think Peter's restoration to Christ impacted his confidence as the lead evangelist on the Day of Pentecost? How does Peter's spiritual journey help us understand what it means to be Spirit-led?

6 Thinking People

Harry Blamires was tutored and encouraged to write by C. S. Lewis at Oxford, and has authored twenty books, mainly on theology, Christianity and society. One of his most articulate and persuasive, *The Christian Mind: How Should a Christian Think?* begins with the startling assertion, 'There is no longer a Christian mind.' The book was written in 1963, when the challenge to traditional Christian beliefs and values had already made a significant impact on society, including the Church, through the secularisation of the Western mind. Blamires speaks of 'secular drift' and 'the loneliness of the thinking Christian', and says:

> 'The Christian mind has succumbed to the secular drift with a degree of weakness and nervelessness unmatched in Christian history.... Everywhere one meets examples of the Church's abdication of intellectual authority which lies at the back of the modern Christian's easy descent into mental secularism.'

Blamires was not alone. Francis Schaeffer's *Escape from Reason* and Jaroslav Pelikan's *The Christian Intellectual* are two among many others with similar views which might be cited. The effects of 'secular drift' – already at work in Peter's day, as reflected in his epistles – and its relevance to End Time people today will become apparent as this chapter unfolds. We shall see that End Time people could not exist then, or at any time, without using their minds.

The Christian mind

In the first chapter of Peter's first epistle he advises believers concerning their minds: 'Therefore gird up the loins of your mind . . .' (1 Peter 1:13). Peter is using an analogy that would have been immediately understood by first-century readers. People at that time wore long, flowing robes which required pulling up and tying around the waist when running or walking quickly. The 1984 edition of the NIV translation of this phrase is very helpful: 'Therefore, prepare your minds for action.' As Barclay says, 'The English equivalent of the phrase would be to roll up one's sleeves, or take off one's jacket. Peter is telling his people that they must be ready for the most strenuous mental endeavour.' It is impossible to miss the importance and timeliness of this admonition to all End Time people. What is also significant is that this emphasis is on the readiness of the mind, and not on the readiness of the body, even though Peter's analogy is about strenuous physical activity. It is a point that should not be missed.

> 'Therefore gird up the loins of your mind . . .' (1 Peter 1:13).

Once again, Peter reflects the rest of New Testament teaching. John's gospel records that Jesus told His disciples that after His departure the Holy Spirit would come and 'teach' them, guiding them to the truth, and that the Spirit would remind them of things He had told them previously (John 14:26 and 16:13). To teach, understand truth, and remember is impossible without use of the mind. Paul also emphasises the importance of the mind when he refers to his own experience: 'I myself in my mind am a slave to God's law' (Romans 7:25, NIV). He speaks of the 'mind of the Spirit' (Romans 8:27), and calls on the believers in Ephesus to 'be renewed in the spirit of [their] mind' (Ephesians 4:23). The author of Hebrews, quoting the Old Testament, declares that God will put His laws into our hearts and minds (Hebrews

> 'I myself in my mind am a slave to God's law.'

10:16). The words in the original Greek of all these texts, *nous* and *dianoia,* mean reason or intellect, the mind at its most basic and essential. To combat eroding secularism, particularly in the Church, Blamires says:

> 'One of the crucial tasks in reconstituting the Christian mind will be to re-establish the status of objective truth as distinct from personal opinions; to rehabilitate knowledge and wisdom in contradistinction from predilection and whim.'

Teaching, truth, knowledge, opinion, wisdom, memory and the capacity to make decisions are all functions of the mind.

Another perceptive writer of the same period, E. L. Mascall, notes in *The Secularisation of Christianity* that even 'well-instructed and thoughtful Christians' can be influenced by 'the intellectual climate and perspectives' of the times in which they live. The 1960s, when Blamires and Mascall and others wrote of their concerns, are widely recognised as a turning point in Western culture, a time of massive and irreversible change in beliefs and values. Dr Martyn Lloyd-Jones, minister at the famous Westminster Chapel in London for nearly thirty years, who also lived at that time, called it 'one of those crucial periods in history when everything seems to be thrown into the melting-pot', with the result 'that the whole of the Christian faith is being rejected and dismissed'. Public opinion, beliefs and morals have never been the same since. Mascall's purpose at the time was the affirmation and communication of the content of 'Christian truth, final, absolute, and fundamentally permanent'.

The process by which the content of Christian truth has been made known is frequently referred to now as *revelation*: that which is divinely revealed, as opposed to the *incomplete, relative and constantly changing* opinions of the surrounding culture. Peter was clearly aware of the fundamental truth of revelation as he wrote his epistles. He uses the words 'revealed' and 'revelation' four times in the eleven verses from 1 Peter 1:3 to 1 Peter 1:13, all with reference to salvation through Christ, who Himself is the ultimate source and purpose of revelation. This process will reach its climax at Christ's coming, referred to by Peter as the salvation 'ready to be revealed on the last day' (1 Peter 1:5, NLT). It is one of the 'absolute and fundamentally permanent' truths in Christian understanding. One wonders what Blamires, Lloyd-Jones and Mascall would have written now, more than half a century later, when insidious and often blatantly anti-Christian secularism continues to run its destructive course.

> 'Prepare your minds for action.'

Peter's appeal to the mind

It will be helpful at this point to return to 1 Peter 1:13 and his admonition to early Christian believers to use their minds in preparation for what lay ahead: 'Prepare your minds for action,' to quote again the 1984 NIV translation. In all translations this phrase is introduced by the word 'therefore' or a similar word such as 'so', as in the 1996 edition of the NLT, which succinctly reads: 'So think clearly.' Peter's advice is the consequence, the logical conclusion, of what has been said in the preceding verses, and can only be fully understood in that context. Christ and His salvation, soon to be fully and finally revealed at His return, are the reason why Peter's readers are advised to 'think clearly'. He is asking them to read verse 13 in the context of verses 3-12, and then to think about it and act on it. It is an implicit appeal to the mind, to the thinking ability of those who will read this epistle, which is what Peter assumes they will do. Rational thought must enlighten belief and initiate behaviour.

Peter writes in this way throughout his epistles, calling for a response to what has just been said, or sometimes to what is about to be said, using the word 'therefore' or a similar word, such as 'for', 'so' or 'since', as the link between what has been said and what follows. So frequent are such passages that it is evident that both epistles have been written with the unspoken assumption that those who read them are expected to use their minds. The following passages all illustrate the point: 1 Peter 1:22-25; 1 Peter 2:1-3, 6-8, 13-16; 1 Peter 4:1-3, 7-10; 1 Peter 5:6-9; 2 Peter 1:5-11, 12-15; 2 Peter 3:14-18. It would be impossible to understand Peter's epistles without thinking clearly and making the logical connection between cause and effect in any of these passages.

One of the above, 2 Peter 1:5-11, is a particularly good

example. Verse 10 begins with 'Therefore', and introduces the admonition: 'Be even more diligent to make your call and election sure.' In verses 5-9, a frequently quoted New Testament passage, Peter speaks about the fruitful growth evident in the life of believers. 'Reason' and 'knowledge' are key words in this passage, the latter appearing five times in verses 2-8. The implication is clear. Growth in the faith and in the Christian virtues results from a knowledge of God and Christ (verse 2), leading ultimately to an 'abundant' entrance into the 'everlasting kingdom of our Lord and Savior Jesus Christ' (verse 11). The words 'reason' and 'knowledge' signify that Peter is again affirming the necessity of using the mind in understanding the implications of faith and in experiencing growth in the Christian life. He then goes on to link knowledge with truth (verse 12). Only a child or a person devoid of any understanding whatsoever could fail to see the implicit assumption in all this – that Peter expects his readers to be capable of rational thought.

> Growth in the faith and in the Christian virtues results from a knowledge of God and Christ.

A similar conclusion can be drawn from the words Peter uses. He assumes that his readers will understand the meaning of words such as 'salvation', 'sanctification', 'obedience', 'sin', 'revelation', 'reason', 'corruptible', and 'incorruptible'. Since words are the basic means of all communication, spoken and written, Mascall says, 'If the Church is to commend its message to those who are outside it, it must speak to them in words that they can understand.' The same is true for those inside the Church. They too must understand what is written as well as what is spoken. It seems clear that Peter understood this, and wrote accordingly, knowing that his readers would make the logical connections necessary to understand his message, and that they would know the meaning of the words he used.

There is one further example of Peter's implicit appeal to the mind. In concluding his second epistle he refers to the epistles of Paul, noting that Paul wrote as a result of the 'wisdom' given to him, and then saying that in Paul's epistles there are 'some things hard to understand' (2 Peter 3:15, 16).

To say that something is hard to understand is not the same as saying it is impossible. It may have been hard for Peter, but that does not mean it was hard for everyone. Paul's epistles were capable of being understood; although, thinking of some passages in Romans perhaps, or in Galatians, many would take Peter's side here! Understanding is always the consequence of careful thought. This is true of all Paul's epistles, as it is of Peter's also. For them to be understood, the mind must be involved, and that is precisely Peter's point here. It is another illustration of his *a priori* assumption that to understand any scripture, his own epistles included, rational thought is required. End Time people, then and now, must use their minds in coming to faith, remaining in the faith, and communicating their faith to others.

End Time people, then and now, must use their minds in coming to faith, remaining in the faith, and communicating their faith to others.

Threats to Christian thinking

There are today two formidable challenges to Christian thinking and to End Time people now, as there were in Peter's day, set out in 2 Peter 2, which we will examine in a later chapter. One threat comes from within the Church, and the other from without. The challenge from without concerns secularism, and the one from within, perhaps surprisingly, relates to the Holy Spirit.

At the beginning of this chapter reference was made to Harry Blamires' book *The Christian Mind*, and to the deleterious effects of secularism on Christian thinking. In a chapter entitled 'The Surrender to Secularism', he says: 'Everywhere one meets examples of the Church's abdication of intellectual authority, which lies at the back of the modern Christian's easy descent into mental secularism,' and goes on to call attention to the 'breadth of the chasm separating the Christian from the secular mind', arguing that the two are distinguished from each other by their conception of truth. The Christian mind is oriented in the supernatural, in divine revelation; the secular mind is rooted in self. 'To think Christianly' (*sic*), Blamires says, 'is to think in terms of revelation':

> 'Briefly, one may sum up the clash between the Christian mind and the secular mind thus. Secularism asserts the opinionated self as the only judge of truth. Christianity imposes the given divine revelation as the final touchstone of truth. . . . Secularism has eaten away from the Christian mind that sense of Revelation's rock-like quality without which the Christian mind is no longer Christian.'

Blamires further comments:

> 'The marks of truth, as "Christianly" conceived, then, are: that it is supernaturally grounded, not developed within nature; that it is objective, and not subjective; that it is a revelation, and not a construction; that it is discovered by enquiry, and not elected by a majority vote; that it is authoritative, and not a matter of choice.'

The concepts of both absolute truth and authority are unacceptable to the secular mind, and the chasm that Blamires noted half a century ago has now grown to an extent unthought of at the time, as has the certainty with which contemporary advocates of secularism proclaim their new gospel. An even more disturbing reality today is that which is conveyed in the title of David Wells' much more recent book, *No Place for Truth, Or Whatever Happened to Evangelical Theology?* already referred to in chapter four. Wells demonstrates that, like a Trojan horse, secularism had already, by the end of the twentieth century, invaded the Church to an astonishing extent. Perhaps worst of all is that there is little chance, he says, if any, of reclaiming the ground that has been lost. It could cogently be argued that this is the most significant concern of all for End Time people today.

We must now turn our attention to the challenge from within, focused on the nature and work of the Holy Spirit. To discuss this matter is like having to walk along a narrow path with dangers lurking on each side. In this case the dangers are, on one side, under-emphasising the work of the Spirit; and, on the other side, over-emphasising that work. Sufficient has been said in the previous chapter to indicate that Peter held and taught a balanced approach to this vital matter, and that in the book of Acts, while miracles were performed by Peter himself and by others, there was nothing irrational or bizarre about the Spirit's work in the early church. Miracles have always been one of the evidences of authentic and credible Christianity, and the miraculous is not contrary to revelation, but compatible with it.

> **There were bodies lying on the floor, having been 'slain by the Spirit'.**

There have been outbreaks of excitement and subjective emotionalism throughout Christian history, which have cast a shadow over the movements themselves, but which have done little harm to Christianity as a whole. That all changed dramatically in 1994 with the outbreak of the Toronto Blessing movement in Toronto, Canada, which quickly spread to the United States, England and other countries around the world. The movement caused much discussion and attracted the attention of other Christian bodies at the time, and its effects are still evident today. Some saw it as a renewal of Christianity; others believed it was hysterical emotionalism and spiritually dangerous. I recall seeing a video of one of the early meetings in Toronto. It was sent to me by someone who thought I would be interested in it because I had recently written a little book about the Holy Spirit entitled *Living in the Spirit*. It did interest me, but I was totally unprepared for what I was about to see. To describe it as an example of extreme charismatic emotionalism at its worst would be an understatement. One critic wrote that 'it obscured reality and enshrined absurdity'. Another described it as 'demonic'.

In a congregation of several hundred, there were bodies lying on the floor, having been 'slain by the Spirit'. Some were seized by uncontrollable laughter, and some were speaking in tongues: not the languages of Acts 2, but an unintelligible gibberish. On the platform, one of the leaders of the meeting was crawling about, barking like a dog. Others were reported to have roared like lions. It can best be described as uncontrolled noisy mayhem, unlike any normal Christian worship service, and totally subjective and self-centred. I would not have believed it if I had not seen it for myself. There is nothing remotely like it recorded by Peter or in the book of Acts. Neither did Jesus say anything about it when He promised that the Holy Spirit would come after His departure (John 14 and 16). He, 'the Spirit of truth', would teach and guide the disciples, and would glorify Christ. It is not surprising that the so-called Toronto Blessing divided Christianity at the time, or that it, or something like it, could do so again.

> The brain cells may be similar, but the authentic Christian mind itself is altogether different.

There is a fundamental relationship in all this with the Christian mind, which is quite different from both the secular mind and the subjective, self-centred and emotionally oriented mind described above. The brain cells may be similar, but the authentic Christian mind itself is altogether different. It is informed, rational, objective, teachable and shaped and led by the 'Spirit of truth', the 'Spirit of Christ', who inspired the prophets of old, predicted the coming of Christ, and undergirded the proclamation of the Gospel which sent the early church on its way (1 Peter 1:11, 12). The Toronto 'blessing' is self-evidently in another category altogether.

Peter's understanding of the mind and its crucial importance reflects the New Testament position as a whole. It is a model for End Time people, then and now. So it is alarming to hear or read of people, especially young people, who appear to have thrown away their minds in favour of a subjective, emotional alternative with far less substance and based on feeling rather than on clear thinking. Such concern is deepened by the fact that in the age in which we live, with its growing and more vocal threats to Christianity, the need for a real Christian mind is now more imperative than ever. That is true for two reasons: for our own sake, and for the sake of the world to which we are called to witness.

Concluding thoughts

Threats and challenges to the Christian mind there are and may yet be, but they must be seen in a right perspective and in the light of normal human and rational thought, as well as from the standpoint of Christian thinking. We began this chapter by referring to the forthright statement of Harry Blamires: 'There is no longer a Christian mind.' We will bring it to a close with another statement from the conclusion of this challenging book, which still speaks strongly to End Time people living today. Referring – in the mid-1960s, let it not be forgotten – to the possibility of a crisis in Western civilisation of a kind not seen before, he says:

'It is better to define, establish and nourish a Christian mind now, as a positive last effort to bring light and hope to our culture, than to have to try and gather together the miserable fragments of Christian consciousness after triumphant secularism has finally bulldozed its way through the Church, as a body of thinking men and women.'

John Stott, the internationally known evangelical Anglican and former rector of All Souls, Langham Place, London, said that Blamires' book *The Christian Mind* was one of the most influential books he had ever read. Stott, himself a prolific and widely read author, is claimed to have influenced more people through his books than Billy Graham did through his preaching. In one of them, *Your Mind Matters: The Place of the Mind in the Christian Life,* Stott discusses several aspects of Christian living, including worship, faith, ministry and evangelism, 'each of which', he says, 'is impossible without the proper use of the mind'. If we have understood Peter correctly, unquestionably he would have agreed.

'He who has an ear, let him hear what the Spirit says to the churches' (Revelation 2:7).

For reflection and further study

1. 'All Word and no Spirit, we dry up; all Spirit and no Word, we blow up; both Word and Spirit, we grow up' (David Watson, *I Believe in the Church*).
2. From your reading of Peter's letters, what evidence do you see to support the notion that Peter understood the necessity of both Word and Spirit for growing in Christ?

Redeemed People

7

The words 'redeem', 'redeemer' and 'redemption' are key words in the Christian vocabulary and are fundamental to Christian teaching and Christian being. They occur more than 150 times in the Bible, in more than thirty books, and are translated from 15 Hebrew and Greek words with various meanings – 'to free', 'to set loose', 'to deliver', 'to separate', 'freedom', and, in one instance, 'the right or price for setting free'. Yet Peter uses only one of these words, 'redeemed', and then only once:

'... knowing that you were not redeemed ['ransomed', ESV] with corruptible things, like silver or gold, from your aimless conduct received by tradition from your fathers, but with the precious blood of Christ, as of a lamb without blemish and without spot' (1 Peter 1:18, 19).

The reason for this apparent inattention to something so basic is that redemption is one of those words, referred to in chapter one of this book, which Peter assumes his readers will understand. They were all Christians, newly converted to Christianity and willing to suffer for their faith if necessary; and, since redemption is of such crucial importance to Christian belief, it would have been impossible for any of them to have become Christian without knowing what that meant.

Edmund Clowney states that in this text Peter comes to the very heart of salvation, saying, 'The way in which Peter speaks of redemption here shows how central it was to the apostolic gospel.' For anyone in the first century to become a Christian, it would have been essential, as it still is today, to understand what redemption was, and that it came through the shed blood of Christ.

Redemption explained and clarified

It might be thought that 'redemption' does not require any explanation. That was not the view of Dr Leon Morris, who, in the introduction to his acclaimed book, *The Apostolic Preaching of the Cross*, said that great biblical words such as 'redemption', 'propitiation' and 'justification' 'mean different things to different people'. Speaking specifically of 'redemption', he says 'it is a term which is employed very loosely' with a 'bewildering variety of meanings in circulation'. He then goes on to write more than fifty pages about 'redemption', its biblical meaning and its historical background. No one who has read the book can doubt that this widely read and meticulous scholar knows what he is talking about. Peter would surely have rejoiced at the title of Dr Morris's book, *The Apostolic Preaching of the Cross*, because that is precisely what he does himself in 1 Peter 1:18 and 19: proclaim the apostolic message about the gospel of redemption.

One of the misunderstandings that Morris comments on is the idea that redemption is the same as salvation. 'Some use it [redemption] as a synonymous term for the whole Christian salvation,' he says. This is a basic misconception. Redemption and salvation, while closely related, are not the same. It is possible to understand the meaning of redemption, even to accept it conceptually, without actually experiencing salvation. But it is not possible to experience salvation without first understanding redemption. Redemption is, as we shall see, a unique, once-only act, rooted in time and history. Salvation is a process, 'the whole Christian salvation', to use Morris's phrase. It will

> It would have been essential, as it still is today, to understand what redemption was, and that it came through the shed blood of Christ.

> Believers have been redeemed 'with the precious blood of Christ, *as of a lamb without blemish and without spot*'.

culminate on the last day, as Peter points out, when he speaks of the 'salvation which is ready to be revealed at the end of time . . . on the Day when Jesus Christ is revealed' (1 Peter 1:5, 7, GNB). Redemption is part of that process, a singular act in time, which in historical terms occurred at Calvary, or which in experiential terms occurs when someone accepts what happened on the cross as meaningful for them, so becoming Christian. Morris concludes his long chapter on redemption, in which he carefully examines the meaning of the original New Testament Greek words, with the modest comment,

> 'Our study has shown . . . that the payment of a price is a necessary component of the redemption idea. When the New Testament speaks of redemption, then, unless our linguistics are at fault, it means that Christ has paid the price for our redemption.'

Peter says that believers have been redeemed 'with the precious blood of Christ, *as of a lamb without blemish and without spot*'. This is a direct reference to the institution of the Passover recorded in Exodus 12:5, when Moses was told to explain to the Israelites that at the beginning of each year every family in Israel was to take a male lamb 'without blemish' as an offering to commemorate their deliverance from Egyptian bondage. The marginal alternative for 'without blemish' is 'perfect'. In the New Testament the Passover and the Passover lamb are referred to as types foreshadowing the death and blood of Christ, as in Mark 14:12 and 1 Corinthians 5:7, whose perfection alone could make His death a redemptive act for all mankind. It is impossible that Peter was unaware of this when he wrote the text quoted above. As Grudem points out, Peter's reference may well include all Old Testament sacrificial offerings which foreshadowed the death of Christ.

The meaning of redemption is further clarified when it is seen in the light of other related biblical words which have similar meanings, or which emphasise a particular aspect of the redemptive act of Christ. We will note here three or four of these words, the first being 'ransom', which, as recorded in Matthew 20:28 and Mark 10:45, Jesus used of His coming sacrificial death. 'Ransom', whether in the form of a noun or verb, is frequently used as a synonym for 'redeem' and 'redemption'. Some biblical word books surprisingly do not even have an entry under 'redemption', but simply a cross reference to 'ransom', or include 'ransom' in their explanation of 'redemption', so close in meaning are the two words. At least three more recent translations of the New Testament, the NLT, ESV and NRSV, use the word 'ransom' or 'ransomed' instead of 'redeemed' in 1 Peter 1:18: for example, 'You know that you were ransomed from the futile ways inherited from your ancestors, not with perishable things like silver or gold, but with the precious blood of Christ' (NRSV). John Murray, in *Redemption Accomplished and Applied*, says,

> 'You know that you were ransomed from the futile ways inherited from your ancestors.'

> 'The language of redemption is the language of purchase and more specifically of ransom. . . . The word of our Lord Himself should place beyond all doubt three facts: (1) that the work He came into the world to accomplish is a work of ransom, (2) that the giving of His life was the ransom price, and (3) that this ransom was substitutionary in its nature.'

The Greek word for 'ransom' is *lutron*, generally translated as 'price', and it refers to the money used to liberate slaves or purchase their freedom. It has been more precisely explained as 'something done for others which they could not do for themselves but which they must have done if they were to have hope'. The ransom price was the death of Christ, resulting in freedom and hope for all who believe. We are reminded of a statement in the book *Desire of Ages*: 'Christ was treated as we deserve, that we might be treated as He deserves.' End Time people have been redeemed, or ransomed, Peter reminds them, by the immeasurably precious blood of Christ. In Clowney's succinct expression, 'His blood is given for our blood.' It is more than a fair transaction.

> The ransom price was the death of Christ, resulting in freedom and hope for all who believe.

It is an unspeakably generous one, never surpassed or equalled in human history.

Two other words with similar meanings are 'reconciliation' and 'atonement', both of which are essential to a full understanding of God's gracious redemptive purposes, and both of which have received much attention from Christian scholars. 'Reconciliation', as described by Paul in Romans 5, refers to a changed relationship, the making of friends between those who were previously estranged, the restoration of a former harmony between two parties. It is described by one writer as follows:

> 'Reconciliation has the significance of a new stage in personal relationships in which previous hostility of mind or estrangement has been put away in some decisive act. . . . Although God looks upon sinful men as enemies, yet He reconciles them to Himself, and has done this by the one decisive act of the cross of Christ.'

It is important here to remember two things. Reconciliation is an act of God towards humankind, not a reaching out to God by men. Taylor says, 'To reconcile is the distinctive activity of God Himself.' Secondly, God's wrath, which results in enmity, is not directed towards human beings, but to sin itself. To think otherwise would be at odds with the most fundamental biblical teaching and the basic Christian belief in the boundless love of God for humankind.

'Atonement' virtually defines itself – 'at-one-ment' – and is, likewise, the act of bringing together those who were formerly estranged. It was through the death of Christ on the cross that atonement was made, and the gulf separating God and humanity was bridged. Again, it came about through the initiative of God, without any human effort or desire. Much time and energy have been spent through the centuries debating the meaning of the atonement. We do not intend to be drawn into that ongoing discussion.

Suffice it to say that 'reconciliation' and 'atonement' are in their outcomes essentially the same. Both were achieved through the death of Christ on the cross; both continue to give freedom, peace and hope to believers; and the effects of both can be seen in the lives of those who are 'in Christ', to use Paul's phrase. Bouttier, quoting 2 Corinthians 5:17 ('if anyone is in Christ, he is a new creation'), says: 'Reconciliation transforms human conduct.' Atonement and reconciliation are truly unique events, rooted in history, but with consequences that will continue to be evident in the lives of all true believers to the end of time.

There is one other word which throws light on the great redemptive act of Christ on the cross. 'Propitiation' occurs only three times in the New Testament, and of them 1 John 4:10 is representative: 'In this is love, not that we loved God, but that He loved us and sent His Son to be the propitiation for our sins.' It seems somewhat strange that John, who writes so much about God's love, should use the word 'propitiation', which carries with it the idea of appeasement, even the appeasement of an angry God. There is, however, a sense in which the wrath of God can be seen as necessary and justifiable, and not merely as an anthropomorphism. Morris speaks of 'a divine hostility to evil' and the 'divine abhorrence of sin', and offers this explanation:

> 'It is the combination of God's deep love for the sinner with His uncompromising reaction against sin which brings about what the Bible calls propitiation . . . (which) signifies the averting of wrath by the offering of a gift. But in both Testaments the thought is plain that the gift which secures the propitiation is from God Himself. He provides the way whereby men may come to Him. Thus the concept of propitiation witnesses to two great realities: the one, the reality and the seriousness of the divine reaction against sin; and the other, the reality and the greatness of the divine love which provided the gift which would avert the wrath from men.'

> It is Christ, not the sinner, who has paid the price, so that He is acting in their stead in His redeeming death.

The death of Christ on the cross can be spoken of too lightly. It is one of the perils of familiarity. The redemption flowing from Christ's death is, in reality, unfathomable, beyond comprehension. The words which the New Testament uses in conjunction with 'redemption' – 'ransom', 'reconciliation', 'atonement' and 'propitiation', among others – help us to understand the depth, the unspeakable mystery, of the cross and God's redemptive intervention in human history.

Those who wish to pursue these themes would do well to read John Stott's classic *The Cross of Christ,* especially chapter seven, 'The Salvation of Sinners', in which he discusses ransom, propitiation, redemption, and reconciliation at some length, but in language that can easily be understood. Stott links propitiation with another essential truth about redemption and atonement: namely, substitution. The idea of substitutionary atonement recurs frequently throughout the quest to understand redemption. It is an idea firmly grounded in Scripture: for example, 2 Corinthians 5:21, 'For God made Christ, who never sinned, to be the offering for our sin' (NLT; see also verse 15). In both 2 Corinthians 5:21 and 2 Corinthians 5:15 the Greek word *huper* is used. Translated 'for', it literally means 'on behalf of' or 'in the place of'. So Morris can say it is Christ, not the sinner, who has paid the price, so that He is acting in their stead in His redeeming death: 'Either He dies or we die.' Stott comments on propitiation and the expiation of sin as related to the substitutionary death of Christ, saying:

> It is this inner condition which lies at the heart of the sin problem, and its solution comes in the form of the redemptive acts of God in Christ.

> 'In Pauline thought, man is alienated from God by sin and God is alienated from man by wrath. It is in the substitutionary death of Christ that sin is overcome and wrath averted, so that God can look on man without displeasure and man can look on God without fear. Sin is expiated and God is propitiated.'

Once again, space prevents us from dealing with any of these themes as they deserve, although much has been written about all of them. The books cited above are only a few of the many that are available.

The necessity of redemption
Peter may or may not have been aware of all the foregoing, but what he emphasises is the necessity of redemption. It is the solution to a problem, the problem of sin. As is the case with many solutions, they cannot be appreciated properly unless the problem is understood in the first place. This is unquestionably true of redemption. Its significance cannot be fully comprehended if the nature of sin is not understood. Peter seems to have grasped this readily. He clearly states that Christ 'bore our sins in His own body on the tree' (1 Peter 2:24), and then proceeds to provide ample evidence of the reality and nature of sin. In the text quoted at the beginning of this chapter, 1 Peter 1:18, he says that redemption was from 'your aimless conduct'. The ESV translates the phrase 'from the futile ways', and the NEB says 'from the empty folly of your traditional ways'. Peter begins chapter two by referring to 'malice, all deceit, hypocrisy, envy, and all evil speaking', and in his second epistle he castigates 'false teachers' who advocate 'destructive heresies' (2 Peter 2:1, 2), pointing out that the Flood came 'on the world of the ungodly' (verse 5), and that Lot was 'oppressed by the filthy conduct of the wicked' (verse 7). He further speaks of the 'pollutions of the world' and of 'the lusts of the flesh' (verses 18, 20), and in chapter three he uses the Flood as an example of the final 'day of judgment and perdition of ungodly men [mankind]' (2 Peter 3:5-7). All this tells us at least two things: that there are sins of the flesh and sins of the mind; and, what may be more important for our purposes, that sin is more than an act or series of acts, sins of commission and omission, but rather an inward condition from which sinful acts and thoughts arise. It is this inner condition which lies at the heart of the sin problem, and its solution comes in the form of the redemptive acts of God in Christ.

Some years ago now I met Dr Lesslie Newbigin – the most courteous, unassuming Christian gentleman one could wish to meet. I have since treasured one of his books, small in comparison to many that have been written about the human condition and God's response to it. The title of Newbigin's book encompasses the entire spiritual saga of humankind in three words: *Sin and Salvation*. It seems that we cannot understand either without the other, and that we have to understand them in that order.

The fact that sin is a condition, a state of being, rather than an act or series of acts (as, for example, in the case of a persistent thief or serial killer) is perhaps the most fundamental truth about sin. Many who have studied the biblical teaching regarding sin have come to the same conclusion. Hans LaRondelle states, 'The root of sin is not found in law-breaking acts themselves, but in a rebellious, self-seeking will.' G. E. Ladd makes a similar comment: 'The root of sin is not found in acts of sinlessness, but in a perverted, rebellious will.' Norman Anderson, a Christian lawyer, explains that 'evil thoughts and deeds . . . well up from the inner being or subconscious mind.' John Stott says, 'The evil things men do originate in their heart.' A murder, a theft, a hateful thought, a desire for revenge, abuse of a child, even a short fuse resulting in the hurt or alienation of someone we love, are all consequences of an innate condition. Any and all of these acts are sinful, but they are not sin itself. Sin is the condition which generates them and every other wrongful thought or act. As someone has rightly said, 'To be human is to be sinful.' A major factor in the conversion of C. S. Lewis, according to one of his biographers, was that 'Lewis looked inside himself and was appalled at what he saw.' Many others have felt the same.

> 'Lewis looked inside himself and was appalled at what he saw.' Many others have felt the same.

Sin also brings guilt, a sense of ill-being, a bad conscience that troubles the perpetrator over things said and done, and also over things not said or done. Guilt can be a terrible burden, a weight which holds down its victims with despair, remorse, even depression, sometimes for months or years. A Google search for poems about guilt is very revealing. There are hundreds of them, from all over the world. This one speaks for thousands:

Redeemed People

> *Stop laughing,*
> *Stop pointing,*
> *Stop staring at me.*
> *Can't you see?*
> *I'm hurt, beaten,*
> *Lying cold on the floor,*
> *With nothing but guilt:*
> *Guilt of having to be me,*
> *Guilt that slowly consumes me,*
> *Guilt which isn't supposed to be within me.*

The consequences of sin are enormous: in this present life; and in every individual life; and, if God's gracious, redemptive work through the death of Christ on the cross is not personally appropriated, then eternally. This is humanity's greatest problem: generally not understood, or forgotten or simply ignored.

End Time people do not just hope that they have been redeemed.

We are now in a position to better understand and appreciate 'redemption', God's solution to the universal human problem of sin, and to grasp the full significance of Peter's assertion that we have been redeemed 'with the precious blood of Christ'. The verb is in the past tense. End Time people do not just hope that they have been redeemed, or that they might have been redeemed, or that one day, perhaps, they will be redeemed. They *know* that they *have been* redeemed, through 'the precious blood of Christ' poured out on Calvary, and not by any other means. It is without question the foundation of their faith; and on this foundation Peter builds everything else he writes to them.

They *know* that they *have been* redeemed, through 'the precious blood of Christ'.

There is another old hymn which is in many hymnbooks and which people still enjoy singing today. It was written by Philip Bliss more than a century ago, and clearly bears witness to an experiential understanding of God's redeeming grace, demonstrated in the death of Jesus. Perhaps that is why it is still popular:

*'Man of Sorrows', what a name
For the Son of God who came
Ruined sinners to reclaim!
Hallelujah! What a Saviour!*

*Bearing shame and scoffing rude,
In my place condemned He stood;
Sealed my pardon with His blood;
Hallelujah! What a Saviour!*

*Guilty, vile, and helpless, we,
Spotless lamb of God was He;
Full redemption – can it be?
Hallelujah! What a Saviour!*

For reflection and further study

What is the difference between the terms 'redemption' and 'salvation', and why is it impossible to understand the meaning of redemption without actually experiencing salvation? And why is it 'not possible to experience salvation without first understanding redemption' (page 75)?

Born-again People 8

Immediately after reminding his readers that they have been redeemed, Peter reminds them of another basic truth which he assumes they have experienced in becoming Christians – that they have also been 'born again':

'Since you have purified your souls in obeying the truth through the Spirit in sincere love of the brethren, love one another fervently with a pure heart, having been born again, not of corruptible seed but incorruptible, through the word of God which lives and abides forever' (1 Peter 1:22, 23).

These verses have generated much comment through the years for several reasons, not least of which is the order in which they appear in the text. It almost seems that they should be reversed, since verse 22 describes what, in effect, are the results of having been born again. The ESV begins verse 23 with 'since', and the NIV with 'for', both indicating that the new birth leads to obedience and brotherly love. After careful consideration of these verses, Wayne Grudem points out, 'The argument is therefore: (1) "love one another earnestly" (verse 22), (2) because "you have been born anew" (verse 23).' We

> 'The argument is therefore: (1) "love one another earnestly" (verse 22), (2) because "you have been born anew" (verse 23).'

shall return later to the consequences of the new birth, but it is necessary to consider first the process of being born again, so fundamental is it in Peter's thinking for End Time people. It is no more possible to be a Christian without being born again spiritually than it is to be a human being without having first been born physically.

The new birth
When Peter speaks of the new birth, which he does twice (in 1 Peter 1:3, 23), he uses a Greek word which no other New Testament writer uses. This word emphasises the fact that the new birth is a second birth. Other translations for the phrase 'having been born again' in verse 23 include 'begotten us again', 'begotten us unto a new life', and 'having been regenerated', the latter giving rise to the more theological word 'regeneration', frequently used synonymously with 'new birth' – as also is 'conversion', another synonym for regeneration. The implication of these translations is that those who have experienced the new birth had already been born naturally before it happened, and that the new birth is a transformation of that which already existed, a radical new beginning, a conversion from what was to what is.

> The new birth is a transformation of that which already existed, a radical new beginning, a conversion from what was to what is.

Peter says that this transforming change came about 'through the word of God', not by any human process which ultimately and inevitably ends in death, but by a divine process which immediately and inevitably results in life. Whether intentionally or unintentionally, this reflects John 1:13, where it is stated that those who believe in Christ become the children of God. They 'were born, not of blood, nor of the will of the flesh, nor of the will of man, but of God'. The new birth is the result of divine activity, as is redemption. It comes about through the creative word of God, and cannot be compared to human procreation. A key phrase in Peter's description of the regenerative process is that the 'word' which initiates the new birth is the 'living and enduring word of God' (1 Peter 1:23, NIV). This cannot have been stated so clearly merely by chance, and it reminds us that Peter, as did all the writers of the Bible, wrote under inspiration, and that what he says about the new birth is ultimately God's word, and not his.

It may legitimately be thought that this creative word includes not only the written word and the spoken word (1 Peter 1:23-25), but also the divine Word Himself, who existed before any words were either written or proclaimed, and whose incarnation provided the context in which John 1:13 was written. The true Word is neither printed, written nor spoken, but is the eternal Word, the divine *Logos,* who was with God in the beginning and who was God, and in whom resided life itself, 'original, unborrowed and underived', who existed before the incarnation and who will exist through all eternity. This is indeed the Word which Peter, under inspiration, describes as 'living and enduring' – that is, alive and eternal (verse 25) – creating new life in those who now come to faith, as He created life in the beginning.

The new birth is divinely conceived, divinely initiated, divinely delivered and divinely perpetuated.

Speaking of Peter's references to the new birth, Barclay says that Christians are people who have been reborn, 'begotten again by God to a new kind of life'. It is a 'change so radical that the only thing that can be said is that life has begun all over again'. Referring to Peter's claim that Christians have been 'begotten . . . again to a living hope' (1 Peter 1:3), he explains:

> 'To the heathen, the world was a place where all things faded and decayed; it might be pleasant in itself, but it was leading to nothing but an endless dark. To the ancient world, the Christian characteristic was hope. . . . He [the reborn Christian] had something of the very seed of God in him, and therefore had in him a life which neither time nor eternity could destroy.'

The new birth is divinely conceived, divinely initiated, divinely delivered and divinely perpetuated.

In the same sentence in which Peter refers to the new birth – almost in the same breath, so to speak – he also mentions the activity of the Spirit (verse 22). In fact, it is the purifying work of the Spirit which is mentioned first. The link here between the new birth and the Spirit is just as obvious as is the link between the new birth and the Word. Both the Word and the Spirit are active in the regenerative process. Mention of the Spirit here also reminds us of the conversation between Jesus and Nicodemus, in which the work of the Spirit in bringing about the new birth is more clearly spelt out than in any other passage of Scripture. The conversation is recorded in John 3:3-8. Jesus said to him:

> 'I say to you, unless one is born again, he cannot see the kingdom of God.... Most assuredly, I say to you, unless one is born of water and the Spirit, he cannot enter the kingdom of God. That which is born of the flesh is flesh, and that which is born of the Spirit is spirit. Do not marvel that I said to you, "You must be born again." The wind blows where it wishes, and you hear the sound of it, but cannot tell where it comes from and where it goes. So is everyone who is born of the Spirit.'

Beyond the imperative 'must be born again', which focuses on the fundamental issue in the conversation, there are two further enlightening facts arising from the original Greek of this passage which deserve our attention. 'Born again' in verse 3 inherently means 'born from above', as the margin again indicates; and 'you' in verse 7 is in the plural, perhaps signifying that Jesus had others in mind besides Nicodemus. Furthermore, the original helps us to grasp an even more important truth – the relationship of the new birth and the kingdom of God. Two different Greek words are used in verses 3 and 5, where Jesus speaks of 'seeing' the kingdom of God and 'entering' it. The word translated 'see' in verse 3 carries with it the meaning of perception and understanding. The truth here is that one must be born again in order to perceive the kingdom of God, to grasp what it means, before one can enter it.

In his book *The Office and Work of the Holy Spirit,* James Buchanan states that there is need of a 'great spiritual change' in the lives of all who would enter the kingdom of God, a change that is implicit in Christ's words, 'You must be born again.' He says: 'The Spirit of God is the author of this change,' and the Word of God is 'the instrument by which the Spirit acts'. There can be little doubt that this is also what Peter is saying: that the new birth is brought about by the activity of the Word and the Spirit together, resulting in that great spiritual change necessitated in all who, like Nicodemus, seek the truth about themselves and about the kingdom of God.

The old life
Peter hints at the nature of this 'great spiritual change' when he reminds believers not to conform themselves any longer 'to the former lusts' (1 Peter 1:14), and when he tells the Church that it is 'chosen', 'a royal priesthood, a holy nation', which once was 'not a people', but is now 'the people of God' (1 Peter 2:9, 10). Put simply, things are different now. Lest there should be any misunderstanding, he comes to the point with a frankness that cannot be misunderstood:

> 'For we have spent enough of our past lifetime in doing the will of the Gentiles – when we walked in lewdness, lusts, drunkenness, revelries, drinking parties, and abominable idolatries' (1 Peter 4:3).

Commenting on this text, Clowney describes the pagan way of life referred to by Peter as 'living in the licentious fast lane', and says that the early Christians addressed here by Peter 'knew well what life in the fast lane was like'. They had been 'Gentile pagans'. There had been wild drinking parties, sexual perversion, idolatrous cults. 'How they would wish to erase those wasted years from their memory,' he adds.

In his second epistle Peter denounces mercilessly the 'false prophets' and 'false teachers' who had infiltrated the Church, pointing out that their lives contradicted any claim they may have had to be speaking the truth. He calls them 'natural brute beasts' who 'speak evil of things they do not understand, having eyes full of adultery' and who 'cannot cease from sin'. They are 'presumptuous' and 'self-willed', 'despise authority', and will

> 'How they would wish to erase those wasted years from their memory.'

'perish in their own corruption'. They are, in a word, totally unregenerate. The picture Peter paints in both epistles of the old, unregenerate life is not a pretty one. It is a sad and salient warning that, however much we may not want to think about it, not all in the Church have been born again. 'By their fruits you will know them,' Jesus said, referring specifically to 'false prophets' who would come in 'sheep's clothing' (Matthew 7:15, 20). Barclay says, 'The point is real, and relevant, and salutary.' The old life described above could well be a summary of the contents of many a popular newspaper or news bulletin in the twenty-first century.

> **Those who live in this way, in the licentious fast lane, 'will not inherit the kingdom of God'.**

Paul also describes the old life in great detail when he counsels the believers in Galatia to 'walk in the Spirit' and not to fulfil 'the lust of the flesh' (Galatians 5:16), specifying the works of the flesh which are anathema and which characterise the life of the unregenerate:

'Now the works of the flesh are evident, which are: adultery, fornication, uncleanness, lewdness, idolatry, sorcery, hatred, contentions, jealousies, outbursts of wrath, selfish ambitions, dissensions, heresies, envy, murders, drunkenness, revelries, and the like . . .' (Galatians 5:19-21).

In saying that those who live in this way, in the licentious fast lane, 'will not inherit the kingdom of God' (verse 21), Paul emphasises what Jesus had told Nicodemus in that memorable conversation which took place at night, probably because Nicodemus was 'a ruler of the Jews' and didn't want his colleagues to know of his quest for truth.

Commenting on the pagan way of life described by Peter and Paul, Clowney also points out that 'the murals of Pompeii reflect the decadence of the Gentile world of Peter's day', which both he and Barclay describe in graphic detail, leaving little to the imagination. Barclay's account reads:

'There was desperate poverty at the lower end of the social scale; but at the top we read of banquets which cost thousands of pounds, where peacocks' brains and nightingales' tongues were served and where the Emperor

Vitellius set on the table at one banquet two thousand fish and seven thousand birds. Chastity was forgotten. Martial speaks of a woman who had reached her tenth husband; Juvenal of a woman who had eight husbands in five years; and Jerome tells us that in Rome there was one woman who was married to her twenty-third husband, she herself being his twenty-first wife. Both in Greece and Rome homosexual practices were so common that they had come to be looked on as natural.'

We are not told how 'husband', 'wife' or 'marriage' were defined, but it probably doesn't matter much. The old life which Peter and Paul condemned so vigorously was essentially pagan, the stark reality of its decadence reflected in the phrase Peter uses when he refers to the lifestyle of the surrounding Gentiles as 'a flood of dissipation' (1 Peter 4:4, NIV 1984).

There is a familiar ring about all this to those who live in the twenty-first century, and who may have read books such as *Slouching Towards Gomorrah* or *How the West Lost God* or *The Death of Christian Culture*. End Time people reading this today may be surprised to find so many parallels with their own day. Maybe they shouldn't be. It is doubtful that either Peter or Paul would have been surprised.

Buchanan notes the scope of this radical change brought about by the new birth when he describes the regenerating work of the Spirit:

'It is not an external reform merely, but an internal and spiritual renovation, a change of mind and heart: taking effect on the understanding, when it is enlightened; on the conscience, when it is convinced; on the will, when it is subdued; on the affections, when they are refined and purified; on the whole man, when "he is transformed by the renewing of his mind" and "created anew in Christ Jesus unto good works"; so that he is said to be "a new creature, in whom old things are passed away, all things have become new".'

> 'It is not an external reform merely, but an internal and spiritual renovation, a change of mind and heart.'

On this more positive note we may now turn our attention to the new life of the believer.

The new life
Beech trees are striking examples of the new life brought about by the new birth. Beeches are large, deciduous trees which grow mainly in the temperate zones of the northern hemisphere, bearing soft green leaves which turn brown in late autumn. The beech is often grown as a thick, low bush, ideal for a garden hedge. There was just such a hedge in the garden of a house where we lived in England, and every autumn the leaves died and turned a rusty brown colour. One winter was particularly harsh, with hard frosts, snow on the ground and on the trees, and gales with strong winds and lashing rain. All through that winter the leaves on the hedge stubbornly stayed put. But spring came eventually, and I can still remember my astonishment when one morning after a calm night I looked out of the window and saw that all the leaves had fallen – the hedge was a bare skeleton of branches and twigs. Then I realised what had happened. The sap had started to rise. New life was flowing through the hedge, and evidence of the old life had gone. So it is with the new life of a Christian, and the most convincing evidence of that new life is that the signs of the old have disappeared.

Peter recognised this. Having just written about 'having being born again' at the end of 1 Peter 1, he begins chapter 2 with 'Therefore'. What follows is the result of the new birth:

'Therefore, laying aside all malice, all deceit, hypocrisy, envy, and all evil speaking, as newborn babes, desire the pure milk of the word, that you may grow thereby' (verses 1 and 2).

In verse 11 of this same chapter he urges new believers to live in a manner which is contrary to the conduct of the pagan Gentiles, and which will bear witness to the fact that they are now God's 'special people', having been called out of darkness

into light (verse 9); and that, as 'sojourners' and aliens in the present world, they should live accordingly. Clowney explains:
'Peter wants Christian pilgrims to remember their heavenly citizenship. Calling his hearers 'transients' or 'pilgrims', Peter returns to a description he used at the beginning of his letter (1:1). He has now shown why they must regard themselves as pilgrims: they are the people of God, a holy nation, and they dare not conform to the wicked conduct of their neighbours. Instead, they must bear witness by their deeds to the kingdom of light.'

> 'Walk in the Spirit, and you shall not fulfill the lust of the flesh.'

Returning to Paul, we note that he writes in similar vein. He urges believers in the Galatian churches to 'walk in the Spirit' (Galatians 5:16), and follows his condemnation of the old life in Galatians 5:19-21 by describing the fruit of the Spirit, implying that those who are led by the Spirit and demonstrate the Spirit's fruits will inherit the kingdom of God:
'I say then: Walk in the Spirit, and you shall not fulfill the lust of the flesh. . . . The fruit of the Spirit is love, joy, peace, longsuffering, kindness, goodness, faithfulness, gentleness, self-control. . . . And those who are Christ's have crucified the flesh with its passions and desires. If we live in the Spirit, let us also walk in the Spirit' (Galatians 5:16, 22-25).

Like the leaves of the beech tree, old habits fall away when new life begins; and when the buds break in the spring and new leaves appear, the new life is evident for all to see.

One of the most compelling examples of new birth and conversion is the experience of John Bunyan, whose life and name are still known after more than three centuries. He is perhaps best remembered for his book, *Pilgrim's Progress*, much of which was written during the twelve years he spent in Bedford's gaol as a prisoner of conscience during the long years of persecution which fell upon non-conformists in the seventeenth century. Among his other books were *The Life and Death of Mr. Badman*, and *Grace Abounding to the Chief of Sinners*, the latter said to be his own spiritual autobiography.

In it he said, 'It was my delight to be taken captive by the Devil at his will,' confessing that he was the ringleader of the local louts and layabouts, 'the youth that kept me company in all manner of vice and ungodliness'. Much of his behaviour was sparked by drunkenness, which continued until he got married.

Bunyan's notoriety as the most profane and dissolute character in the community was later matched by a reputation for sobriety and godliness – perhaps the most convincing example that age provided, and there were many, of that improbable transformation which could become a reality in ordinary human experience. It was, without doubt, one of the most remarkable conversions to which the pages of English religious history still bear testimony.

There is a much-loved hymn, translated in 1867 from a fifteenth-century Italian source, and set to a beautiful tune by Ralph Vaughan Williams, whose words sum up all that has been said above about the Holy Spirit who initiates, creates and sustains the new life of the born-again believer:

> *Come down, O Love divine, Seek Thou this soul of mine,*
> *And visit it with Thine own ardour glowing;*
> *O Comforter draw near, within my heart appear,*
> *And kindle it, Thy holy flame bestowing.*
>
> *O let it freely burn, till earthly passions turn*
> *To dust and ashes in its heat consuming;*
> *And let Thy glorious light shine ever on my sight,*
> *And clothe me round, the while my path illuming.*
>
> *Let holy charity mine outward vesture be,*
> *And lowliness become my inner clothing;*
> *True lowliness of heart which takes the humbler part,*
> *And o'er its own shortcomings weeps with loathing.*

And so the yearning strong, with which the soul will long,
Shall far outpass the power of human telling;
For none can guess its grace, 'til he become the place
Wherein the Holy Spirit makes His dwelling.

That this is indeed a reality and a possibility, as emphasised by Peter and other New Testament writers, has been experienced literally by millions of new believers through the centuries. It is still the hope and prayer of all true End Time people.

For reflection and further study

Shaky Simon – the disciple of Christ – became rock-solid Peter – the apostle of Christ. Describe his transformation from the young Galilean fisherman to Peter, the mature church leader. How does his life story help us understand what it means to be 'born again'?

9 People who Grow

There is an ambiguity in the title of this chapter concerning the people who 'grow'. Does it mean that Peter wrote about the growth of the Church as a whole, or the growth of individual believers? Is he concerned with congregational growth, or with personal growth? While there is clearly a relationship between the two, there is also a distinction. The Church can grow as congregations increase, and a congregation can grow in numbers without all its members growing spiritually in the Christian life. This is an important caveat, and we will return to it shortly. But first we pause to note a comment made by Michael Green in the preface to his commentary on 2 Peter about the relevance of Peter's epistles in general.

What Peter says is relevant both to early Christians and to all who would come later until the last day finally arrives.

After stating that both epistles 'carry a very important message for our times', Green writes:

'We live in days when the contents of the Christian faith are widely questioned, when new and speculative theologies are widely disseminated, and when a new morality is being advocated which is capable of being misunderstood as "the old immorality writ large". . . . There is, moreover, an intellectualism about much of our Christianity which is not, perhaps, so far removed from that attacked in these letters – the knowledge that has little relation to holy living, growing spiritually and deepening love.'

Green's commentary relates primarily to the early Christians in Asia Minor to whom Peter was writing: 'aliens' living in a foreign land, but bound for a new and better country. Green's message, however, is that what Peter says is relevant both to early Christians and to all who would come later until the last day finally arrives. This applies as much to what he says about growth as it does to everything else he wrote. Perhaps more importantly, it also addresses the concern which led to this book, as explained in Chapter 1: the cerebral attachment to last-day events without the spiritual response required in daily living and readiness for the coming of Christ . . . in short, the kind of people End Time people should be.

The nature of growth
We may now return to the question of what Peter says about growth. He speaks about it three times – in 1 Peter 2:2; 2 Peter 1:5-7; and 2 Peter 3:18. The text in 1 Peter 2 is key to what he says later in the second epistle, which begins and ends on the theme of growth. It might understandably be thought that Peter's primary interest would be the growth of the many congregations which had sprung up across Asia Minor even before he wrote his letters, and to which 1 Peter in particular is specifically addressed. He had heard Jesus deliver the 'great commission' recorded in Matthew 28, and understood well the mission of the Church. He could not but be interested in the welfare of these scattered groups of believers, as his epistles demonstrate at many points.

There are, however, several reasons to think that when in 1 Peter 2:2 Peter encourages growth, he is primarily concerned with the spiritual growth of believers rather than congregations. If the believers themselves were to grow, then the growth of the Church and its congregations would take care of itself. Firstly, we should note carefully the passage in question, 1 Peter 2:1, 2 – notably verse 1, which begins with

'Therefore', indicating again that what follows is a consequence of what has just been said previously – namely, that these believers have been born again:

'Therefore, laying aside all malice, all deceit, hypocrisy, envy, and all evil speaking [marks of the old life], as newborn babes, desire the pure milk of the word, that you may grow thereby' (1 Peter 2:1, 2).

Because they have been born again to a new life, they are to lay aside evidence of the old life, and, as 'newborn babes', proceed to grow, as discussed in the previous chapter. The process of rebirth takes place inwardly and individually. Congregations are not reborn *en masse.* So now Peter urges these believers to grow as newborn babies grow, naturally, towards adulthood and maturity.

Secondly, 2 Peter 1:5-7, which has been called 'the ladder of faith' – and indeed the entire passage, verses 5 to 11, which in the NKJV has the subheading, 'Fruitful Growth in the Faith' – reads more easily if it is thought of as being personal rather than congregational. 'Self-control', 'diligence', and 'perseverance', for example, are aspects of growth which are more readily understood as personal qualities or individual traits of character. Green says that this passage contains a 'list of virtues which should be found in a healthy Christian life', and notes Peter's use of the personal pronouns 'he' and 'his', rather than 'them' and 'theirs', in verse 9.

Thirdly, verse 10 urges diligence in making 'your call and election sure' – clearly choices that can only be made by the individuals concerned. The preceding verse, verse 9, mentions the blindness of the one who 'has forgotten' that he was cleansed from his 'old sins', a reference to the time of 'his' first belief, something that would not ordinarily be said in that way to a gathered congregation. Commenting on this text, one commentator says, 'A life of steady progress should characterise the Christian.'

Finally, this whole passage concludes in verse 11, which commences with the words 'for so'.

The Greek here means 'under these circumstances' or 'furthermore', and again refers back to all that has been said from verse 5 to this point. Consequently, God will, as J. B. Phillips paraphrases it, 'open wide to you the gates of the eternal kingdom'. Again, it must be said that entrance to the kingdom does not depend on belonging to this church or to that congregation, but on personally understanding and accepting all that Peter has said in this remarkable passage. Michael Green says of verse 11, 'The noblest description of heaven is in personal categories like this. It will embody utterly harmonious relationships between the Saviour and the saved.' A congregation should be an assembly of individual believers, all born again and now growing.

> He could not have stressed the importance of continuing growth more emphatically. It is not an option, but a necessity.

It seems, then, quite clear that Peter's chief concern is the growth of believers. Continuing personal growth in faith, knowledge, understanding and the Christian virtues, and the internalisation of all that Peter has recommended, is the way to the kingdom. This does not exclude congregational growth, but rather makes it possible.

The necessity of growth

Some of Peter's last words to his readers, written shortly before the end of his life and probably from his prison in Rome, were about growth: 'But grow in the grace and knowledge of our Lord and Savior Jesus Christ' (2 Peter 3:18). It is one of the most quoted texts from Peter, and deservedly so. Of all the things Peter could have said as he came to the end of his life and his letters – perhaps about the nearness of Christ's coming, or about faith, or hope, or godly living, for example – he exhorts them to grow in grace and in Christ. It is, in fact, more than exhortation. The Greek verb 'to grow' is in the present imperative, 'Grow ye.' He could not have stressed the importance of continuing growth more emphatically. It is not an option, but a necessity.

By this point, at the end of his second epistle, Peter has already warned of false teachers arising from within, and of the 'many' who would 'follow their destructive ways'. He also warns of the possibility that after having 'escaped the pollutions of the world through the knowledge of the Lord and Savior Jesus Christ', it is possible to again become 'entangled in them and overcome' (2 Peter 2:20). It is quite likely that he had seen for himself evidence of the havoc these imposters had already caused. There is more than a hint of that in the penultimate verse of chapter three, where he counsels his readers to 'beware lest you also fall . . . led away with the error of the wicked' (verse 17).

> The Christian life is like riding a bicycle: 'Unless you keep moving, you fall off.'

Commenting on Peter's final words in verse eighteen, Green says that the Christian life is like riding a bicycle: 'Unless you keep moving, you fall off,' adding, 'It is a developing life, for it consists in getting to know at even greater depth an inexhaustible Lord and Saviour.' Barclay says that in the Christian life 'there must be steady moral advance', and cites a comment made by James Moffatt that has been noted by more than one commentator: 'The Christian life must not be an initial spasm followed by chronic inertia.' A modern cynic could be forgiven for thinking that that is often what it appears to be at times, both from a congregational standpoint as well as in reflecting on one's own experience. A good dose of Peter could be the cure, and that is one of the reasons this book has been written. The author testifies to the efficacy of the medication, and has come to see that more than one dose is necessary.

The 'fruitful growth' which Peter advocates at the beginning of 2 Peter 1 calls for further consideration. Thoughtful reading of verses 5-7 – which has been called, perhaps a little unfortunately, the 'Ladder of Faith' – raises a number of questions:

- Are all these virtues or characteristics of the Christian life to be seen fully developed in the life of every believer, regardless of age or circumstance? What about those who die at a young age, or as the result of persecution, and do not have the opportunity to reach maturity, either physical or spiritual?
- Are there no other Christian virtues which are equally as

important as those which Peter lists – honesty, patience, forgiveness, and faithfulness, for example, many of which are mentioned elsewhere in the New Testament as indications of growth?
- Is Peter's list a sequence which must be followed strictly in the order he sets out? Some people are born with innate tendencies to some of these traits. They are by nature patient or honest or self-denying. It would surely be superfluous for them to add qualities they already possessed.
- Does Peter intend that all who read this epistle should proceed to add these virtues to their faith at the same pace? Surely not. Potential Christians have not been programmed to grow in unison.

It may not be possible to answer all these questions definitively, or some of them even at all. They nonetheless require constant reflection by all who have begun to climb this ladder.

The so-called 'Ladder of Faith' has also been called 'The Upward Way'. Perhaps that is a better description. A ladder is used to climb to the top of something in order to reach a goal or complete a task. Maybe there is more than one route up to the Celestial City which Bunyan had Pilgrim reach. Green says that Peter's list 'illustrates the way in which the Christian life must be worked out in behaviour'. Perhaps the best way to regard Peter's list is to see it as an example of the kind of growth that is to be experienced by every Christian who has been born again and is on his or her way to the kingdom.

Barclay summarises the passage we have been considering in his usual thoughtful way:

'Peter strongly urges his people to keep climbing up this ladder of virtues which he has set before them. The more we know of any subject, the more we are fit to know. . . . Progress is the way to more progress. Moffat says of ourselves and Jesus Christ: "We learn of Him as we live with Him and for Him." As the hymn puts it:

> **Peter's list 'illustrates the way in which the Christian life must be worked out in behaviour'.**

'May every heart confess Thy name,
And ever Thee adore,
And, seeking Thee, itself inflame
To seek Thee more and more.'

The bottom line in all this is that growth in the Christian life is both essential and possible.

> 'If you do these things, you will never stumble, and you will receive a rich welcome into the eternal kingdom of our Lord and Saviour Jesus Christ.'

How, then, do we grow?
This is another important question, the answer to which is both challenging and comforting. We must here return to the 'Upward Way', which leads ultimately to the kingdom (verse 11). At the beginning of this passage, in verse 5, as noted already, Peter admonishes believers to 'add' a sequence of qualities which, if developed, will ensure that those who possess them will be useful and fruitful in the Christian life they have just espoused. 'Adding' is another function of the mind which requires mental effort in order to result in a quantifiable outcome. The NIV translation of verses 8 to 11 is enlightening:

'For if you possess these qualities in increasing measure, they will keep you from being ineffective and unproductive in your knowledge of our Lord Jesus Christ. . . . For if you do these things, you will never stumble, and you will receive a rich welcome into the eternal kingdom of our Lord and Saviour Jesus Christ.'

The NIV notes that in the phrase 'in increasing measure', 'Peter has continuing spiritual growth in mind.' Similarly, the wording of 1 Peter 2:1 uses the term 'laying aside', again indicating effort on the part of these newborn Christians that they may grow. To quote Green once again, he says of 2 Peter 1:5, 'The grace of God demands, as it enables, human effort in man. . . . Human effort is indispensable, even though it is inadequate.'

A packet of seeds will illustrate the point. Any packet will do. I am looking at a packet of radish seeds, which promises radishes that are 'crisp and crunchy'. But there is not the slightest possibility that these seeds will grow unless the instructions on the packet are carried out: 'thin out', 'water well', 'dig in plenty of organic matter'. Only action on the part of the sower will yield 'crisp and crunchy' radishes. Christ's parable of the sower begins with the words, 'Behold, a sower went out to sow' (Matthew 13:3). The sower got up one morning, picked up the seed, put it in a bag, grabbed whatever tools he needed, then walked out to the field and scattered it on the ground. In fact, six separate actions were required by the sower in order to produce a crop. G. Campbell Morgan, commenting on this parable, quotes from a writer who had been to Palestine and seen a sower in action:

> 'The sower, in the days of our Saviour, lived in a hamlet or village; he did not sow near his own house.... He must go forth into the open country... where thorns grow in clumps all around; where rocks peep out in places through the scanty soil; and where, also, are patches extremely fertile. ... That man, with his mattock, is digging in places where the rock is too near the surface for the plough.'

It is easy to visualise such a man, working a small patch of land on the verge of scrub, as he toils under the hot sun in an effort to get the seeds to grow to harvest. Some might think it a lot of effort for little reward. They would probably be right!

Peter enjoins us to 'add' that we may 'be neither barren nor unfruitful' (2 Peter 1:5, 8); to be 'laying aside' that we 'may grow thereby' (1 Peter 2:1, 2); to 'abstain from fleshly lusts which war against the soul' (1 Peter 2:11); and, using the imperative, to 'grow' (2 Peter 3:18). Herein is the challenge to Christian growth. The challenge may be difficult at times, and seemingly relentless. Without question, it requires effort – even though, as Green rightly says, human effort 'is inadequate' of itself.

> **Without question, it requires effort – even though, as Green rightly says, human effort 'is inadequate' of itself.**

It might be objected that this suggests salvation by works, contradicting the basic principles of Protestantism: *sola gratia* (by grace alone) and *sola fide* (by faith alone). That would be true if we were considering justification. However, we are considering another dimension of salvation, sanctification; and, although the two are inseparably related, they are quite distinct. There cannot be full salvation without both justification and sanctification; and it is to the latter that we now turn, for therein lies comfort.

Sanctification and the Spirit

In this chapter we are seeking to understand what Peter wrote about sanctification and holiness in the process of Christian growth. Sanctification can only be fully understood in the light of everything the New Testament says about it; and, even then, the subject will remain a source of debate, and, at times, not a little confusion. Furthermore, it may appear that there is some repetition in this chapter of what has been said in earlier chapters: but, since sanctification is a major factor in Christian growth, some repetition is inevitable if we are to fully understand Peter's concerns and their relationship to each other. And, in any case, a little repetition does wonders for the memory.

> One can be 'set apart' without being holy, but cannot be holy without being set apart.

Peter uses the verb 'sanctify' and the noun 'sanctification' once each (1 Peter 1:2 and 3:15). As noted previously, these words come from two related Greek words, *hagiazo* and *hagiasmos*, both having the basic meaning of 'setting apart', but also having the connotation of holiness. Lowe says that the noun 'sanctification' applies 'both to an experience of being set apart for God, and to the believer's subsequent manner of life'. Peter also uses another word much more frequently, *hagios*: also meaning 'set apart', but which also carries the sense of holiness. The close relationship of being 'set apart' and being 'holy' is self-evident, as is the fact that there is also a difference. Again, as noted previously, one can be 'set apart' without being holy, but cannot be holy without being set apart.

Peter uses *hagios* no fewer than ten times: more than enough to show how important the idea of holiness was in his thinking. He speaks of a 'holy God', a 'holy nation', 'holy conduct', 'holy men', 'holy prophets', and, of course, the 'Holy Spirit', the divine Agent active in the process of sanctification.

P. S. Watson, speaking of sanctification, reminds us that it is:
> '. . . not fully accomplished within the limits of our present life, much less in the first moment of our Christian existence. Nor is it something we can achieve ourselves. It is the work of God's grace, brought about by the Holy Spirit.'

A key text in Peter's epistles is 1 Peter 1:15: 'But as He who called you is holy, you also be holy in all your conduct,' and this injunction is followed up with another reminder: 'You are . . . a holy nation, His own special people, that you may proclaim the praises of Him who called you out of darkness into His marvelous light . . . having your conduct honorable among the Gentiles' (1 Peter 2:9, 12). Holiness is not an end in itself, nor only an inner personal experience. It is intended to reflect the holiness of God to the unbelieving Gentiles: and there are plenty of them around today, as there were in Peter's day.

There are two dangers inherent in the process of sanctification: the first – again, as noted previously – being the idea that it leads ultimately to perfection. It has been pointed out that those who are called 'saints' in the church 'are not flawless paragons of virtue', but are 'beset by innumerable infirmities and are liable to all kinds of mistakes as long as they live'. The other danger is the possibility that it will lead to a sense of self-righteousness, the insidious feeling that one is better than others, especially the unbelieving 'Gentiles'. The Dutch theologian G. C. Berkouwer reminds us that the unbeliever may detect in the Christian pursuit of sanctification 'a presumptuous note, the pretension of being saintly', a perception which will deter rather than attract. He adds that true sanctification 'shuns theatrical piety'.

> 'You are . . . a holy nation, His own special people, that you may proclaim the praises of Him who called you out of darkness into His marvelous light.'

The response to both these possibilities is that genuine sanctification is not solely the result of personal effort, however diligent or sincere it may be, but that it is the work of the Holy Spirit. Many books and articles have been written through the years by different authors from different perspectives about sanctification and holiness, yet they demonstrate a remarkable consensus. The Holy Spirit is the energising, enabling Agent in the sanctifying process: 'The Holy Spirit is a sanctifying agency'; 'Sanctified by the Spirit'; 'The process of sanctification by the Spirit'; 'The sovereign work of the Holy Spirit'; 'Holiness . . . which the Spirit effects in us'; 'The work of God, more especially of the Holy Spirit'; 'Progressively sanctified . . . as we are possessed by the Holy Spirit'. There are many other such comments which could be cited. They all tell us that we are not alone as we walk the upward path to the celestial city; nor do we have to rely on our own inadequate strength.

> The Holy Spirit is the energising, enabling Agent in the sanctifying process.

Christ promised the coming of the Paraclete – 'Comforter', 'Helper', 'Sanctifier', 'Guide', 'Enlightener', 'Enabler', the third Person of the Godhead, God Himself indeed, the divine, powerful and indispensable Agent of sanctification and the unfailing catalyst of holiness and Christian growth. The comforting truth is that we do not need to wait for the Spirit who is yet to come, but to receive and submit to Him who is already here, willingly and daily. Three hundred years ago, Isaac Watts wrote a hymn which has been sung ever since by sincere, struggling Christians who walk the narrow way to the kingdom. It is a prayer for help, a recognition that we cannot travel alone, and an assurance that it is possible to reach our final destination, despite all the trials and difficulties we might face:

Come, Holy Spirit, heavenly Dove,
With all Thy quickening powers;
Kindle a flame of sacred love
In these cold hearts of ours.

O raise our thoughts from things below,
From vanities and toys!
Then shall we with fresh courage go
To reach eternal joys.

For reflection and further study

'But grow in the grace and knowledge of our Lord and Saviour Jesus Christ' (2 Peter 3:18, NIV). What does it mean to grow in 'grace and in Christ'? When Peter talks of 'grace', what does he mean?

10 People with Faith

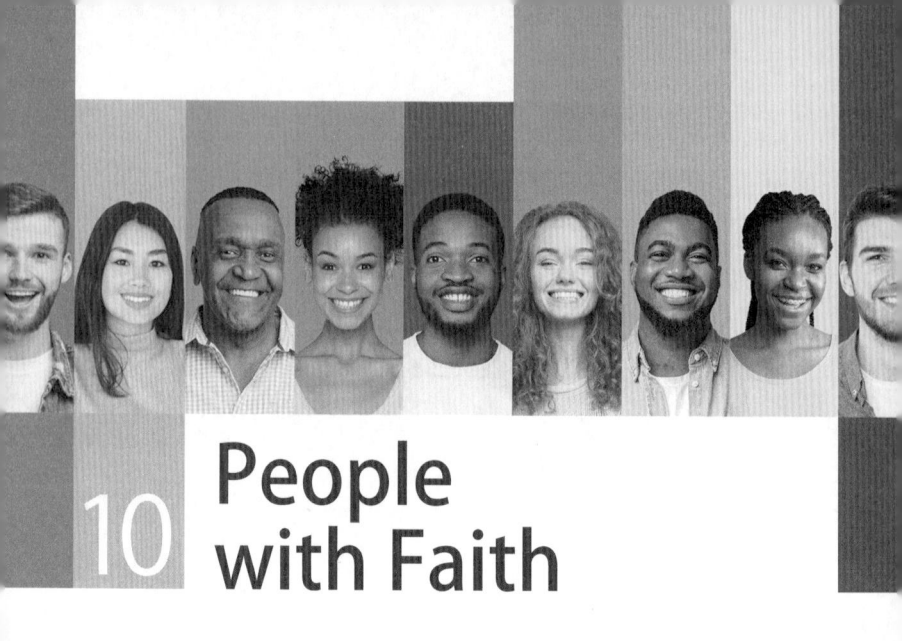

It might be thought unnecessary for Peter to say that End Time people had faith. They were all believers, having come out of dark paganism or legalistic Judaism to become Christians, and in so doing had accepted Christ, putting their faith in Him as Redeemer and Lord. Without faith they would not and could not have become Christians and Peter would not have written his epistles to them, encouraging and instructing them in their new-found faith. Faith is unconditionally foundational. It is the very first fundamental, the *sine qua non*, of authentic Christian belief and the Christian way of life. 'For by grace you have been saved through faith' (Ephesians 2:8), and 'without faith it is impossible to please Him' (Hebrews 11:6).

The word 'faith' is used in twenty-six of the twenty-seven books of the New Testament, more than 230 times in all. The Greek word in all these texts is *pistis,* beautifully defined in Souter's *Lexicon to the Greek New Testament* as 'faith, belief, trust, the leaning of the entire human personality upon God . . . in absolute trust and confidence in His power, wisdom, and goodness'. John is the only gospel writer not to use *pistis* (with the English

> Faith is unconditionally foundational. It is the very first fundamental, the *sine qua non*, of authentic Christian belief.

translation 'faith'), using instead the related Greek verb *pisteuo* ('I believe' or 'to believe'), of which Lowe rightly says, 'There is really no distinction between "faith" and "belief" in the Greek New Testament.' The same applies, of course, to English translations.

Peter uses both 'faith' and 'believe', but only nine times in all, equivalent to about 3% of the entire New Testament usage. It could be reasonable to think that such sparing use of these fundamental words indicates that he does not regard faith as highly as he ought to, or perhaps as highly as we think he should: but that would be a mistake. By the time Peter wrote his epistles in the early to mid-60s AD, much of the New Testament had already been written; and, as suggested in a previous chapter of this book, he would have been aware of much of the New Testament teaching about faith, as well as other aspects of Christian belief. To conclude that he did not value faith would be a serious error of judgement. In all nine references to faith or belief, he says something valuable to the new Christians of the first century, and to all Christians who would later read his letters. It would be more accurate to think that Peter assumes his readers understand the basics of faith as he himself does, and that he builds on what other New Testament writers have said, and on what his early readers already know and try to practise. We must avoid putting words into Peter's mouth, so to speak, and focus on what he said, rather than on what he did not say. As we shall see, there is enlightenment and depth in what Peter says that is as fresh today as it was when first written.

There is enlightenment and depth in what Peter says that is as fresh today as it was when first written.

The necessity of faith

It might also appear superfluous to stress the necessity of faith in the Christian life. There is another word, however, which comes to mind when considering the necessity of faith; and, although similar in meaning, there are important shades of difference. It is the word 'primacy'. In fact, it might be more appropriate to use 'primacy' instead of 'necessity', since that which has primacy is also on that account necessary. Be that as it may, there are two important texts in Peter where both the necessity and the primacy of faith become evident: 1 Peter 1:5 and 2 Peter 1:5. Considered together, they make Peter's comments about faith some of the most enlightening in the New Testament.

In the first of these texts Peter affirms that God's pilgrim people, on their way to the kingdom, are 'kept by the power of God through faith for salvation'. This salvation – again, as noted previously, and as the text makes plain – was already, in Peter's day, 'ready to be revealed in the last time' – or, as the NLT puts it, 'on the last day' – and it was imminently expected. The ultimate reward for Christian believers is in sight, despite trials, persecution and isolation. We can see the light at the end of the tunnel, and Peter's message is that God will keep His people 'through faith', so that they will be ready to witness the climax of salvation at the last day and be ready to receive it.

> **The ultimate reward for Christian believers is in sight, despite trials, persecution and isolation. We can see the light at the end of the tunnel.**

Commenting on this text, Grudem says, 'God's power does not work apart from the personal faith' of believers, but 'through their faith'. This individual, personal faith is 'the means' God uses to guard His people as they wait for the last day and 'the final, complete fulfilment of their salvation'. First Peter 1:5, in the context of the passage in which it is set (verses 3-12), makes it abundantly clear that the salvation which is shortly to be revealed is found in and through Christ, who is the fulfilment of Old Testament Messianic prophecies (verses 10-12). He is the source of salvation, and faith in Him will carry the believer through until 'the revelation of Christ' at the end of days.

The entry on faith in *Vocabulary of the Bible* affirms what Peter says about salvation, faith and the coming climactic revelation of Christ:

'The proper object of faith, according to the New Testament, is Jesus Christ, who is the revealer of God, who brings salvation to its fruition in His name, and who, uniting believers to Himself, unites them to God and saves them. ... In his act of belief the Christian says "Yes" and "Amen" to the message of Jesus. ... He knows that with the life, death and resurrection of Jesus the history of salvation has entered into the last epoch and is to reach its term "at the last day" with the return of Christ. ... Faith gives life and salvation.'

The other text in which Peter affirms the primacy and necessity of faith is 2 Peter 1:5. This brings us back to the 'Ladder of Faith' or 'The Upward Way', which was commented on in the previous chapter when considering Christian growth. Peter again assumes that his readers have faith and that they understand what it means. He then enjoins them to 'add' to their faith a sequence of virtues which are self-evidently characteristic of the Christian life. It is not necessary to repeat what was said in chapter 9, except perhaps to point out that faith is the starting point from which the believer is to grow by adding to it the virtues which follow. Without faith, there could be no 'Upward Way' leading to the kingdom, nor any 'Ladder' stretching heavenward. In this setting, faith can be likened to a ladder placed on solid ground, enabling upward progress and which will not give way. To change the analogy, as Green has said, 'Faith is the foundation stone on which the virtues which follow are built.' Like a building reaching skyward, it must rest on a sure foundation, without which it would collapse.

Lenski likens the virtues which Peter lists to 'seven jewels, all of them fastened to faith'. Faith is not one of the 'jewels', but the 'golden chain' to which the jewels are attached. Without the chain, the jewels would be scattered, possibly lost and worthless. He also notes that in Peter's text believers already have faith, on account of the Gospel they have accepted. Now they must 'add' to their faith. Barclay stresses the personal element in faith, saying that everything goes back to *pistis,* adding that, for Peter, 'Faith is the conviction that what Jesus Christ says is true, and that we can commit ourselves to His promises and launch ourselves on His demands.' He also points out that the

> 'Faith is the foundation stone on which the virtues which follow are built.'

Greek word translated 'Add' at the beginning of verse 5 has the note of an imperative, and therefore is not optional; and that it can be translated 'equip yourselves', throwing yet more light on the faith that Peter has in mind: not a blind or passive faith, but one which enjoins action and initiative. Perhaps words from Daniel Whittle's hymn written in 1883 fairly summarise how crucial faith has been and still is on the Upward Way:

> *I know not how this saving faith to me He did impart,*
> *Nor how believing in His word*
> *wrought peace within my heart.*
> *But I know whom I have believed,*
> *and am persuaded that He is able*
> *To keep that which I've committed unto Him against that day.*

> Avoid controversy and those who teach false doctrine, striving instead to promote love, which comes 'from a pure heart'.

The nature of faith

Faith is usually thought of positively, as the foregoing comments indicate. Yet Peter sounds a note of caution when he expresses the hope that the faith of his readers 'may be proved genuine' (1 Peter 1:7, NIV 1984). There is a suggestion here that faith may not always be genuine: that in fact it may be feigned or insincere. This hint of insincerity echoes the advice of Paul to Timothy that he should avoid controversy and those who teach false doctrine, striving instead to promote love, which comes 'from a pure heart, from a good conscience, and from sincere faith' (1 Timothy 1:4, 5). The possibility of insincere faith is here raised again. The older King James Version uses the expression 'faith unfeigned'.

The English word 'sincere' comes from the Latin *sincerus* or *sine cerus*, meaning literally 'without wax', and is usually translated as 'genuine' or 'unmixed'. It is said that in the days of the Roman Empire unscrupulous traders would use wax to plug holes or cracks in products such as furniture or other damaged goods which were for sale. When the wax had hardened, it would be painted over and the article sold as new and unblemished. Those that were authentic, undamaged, would be declared *sine cerus*, without wax – that is, genuine.

Similarly, genuine faith is sincere, uncontaminated by self-interest or self-advancement, unfeigned.

Peter also mentions faith in two other texts in 1 Peter 1. In verse 8 he commends the young Christians to whom he is writing for 'believing' in Christ even though they have not seen Him, and in verse 21 he states that they 'believe in God'. This phrase opens the door to alternative interpretations: that they believe in Him in the sense that they trust Him, or in the sense that they believe He exists. We are reminded of Hebrews 11:6, where Paul states that those who come to God must 'believe that He is' – that is, must believe that He exists. Only those who believe that He exists can come to Him for help. He must *be* before He can *act*. Belief in His existence is an intellectual conviction; belief that He rewards those who seek Him is an act of faith. Intellectual assent does not necessarily lead to personal faith. Commenting on this text, Barclay notes, 'There are many who believe in God, but do not believe that He cares.'

> Those who come to God must 'believe that He is' – that is, must believe that He exists.

These two kinds of faith may be described as 'faith *that*' and 'faith *in*'. Faith *that* is not saving faith, although it is a step in the right direction. There are many examples of faith *that* which do not go far enough. Faith *that* God exists, *that* Christ was the Son of God, *that* the Bible is God's word, do not of themselves necessarily indicate that those who so believe put their trust in God, or in Christ, or in the Bible. Of the relationship between faith and works James says, 'You believe that there is one God. Good! Even the demons believe that – and shudder' (James 2:19, NIV). Barclay explains:

> Faith *that* is impotent to save of itself. It must be accompanied by faith *in*. When Peter uses the word 'faith' he almost invariably means the latter.

> 'What James is arguing against is the first kind of belief, the acceptance of a fact without allowing it to have any influence upon life. The devils are intellectually convinced of the existence of God: they, in fact, tremble before Him; but their belief does not alter them in the slightest.'

Faith *that* is impotent to save of itself. It must be accompanied by faith *in*. When Peter uses the word 'faith' he almost invariably means the latter. He had witnessed the power of faith in those early days after Pentecost when faith in Jesus had healed the cripple at the gate of the Temple, as recorded in Acts 3:16.

> **There must be conviction of God, but there must also be a relationship with Him.**

Grudem helpfully points out that 1 Peter 1:7, where Peter refers to the 'genuineness' of the faith of early Christians, can only be fully understood in context. Having noted in verse 6 that they 'have had to suffer grief in all kinds of trials' (NIV), Peter writes:

> '. . . that the genuineness of your faith, being much more precious than gold that perishes, though it is tested by fire, may be found to praise, honor, and glory at the revelation of Jesus Christ.'

Grudem then comments, 'The trials burn away any impurities in the believer's faith. What is left is purified, genuine faith, analogous to the pure gold or silver that emerges from the refiner's fire.' Faith in the sense of complete trust – faith *in* – leads the believer to the salvation that will be finalised at the coming of Christ. Faith *that* together with faith *in* is saving faith, genuine and 'without wax'.

Few have written about true faith with more conviction and clarity than Dr G. Campbell Morgan, formerly the minister at the Westminster Chapel in London and principal of Cheshunt College, Cambridge, England. He was known worldwide as one of the leading biblical expositors of his day, and the author of more than eighty books, many of which have become classics in biblical exposition. In *The Parables and Metaphors of our Lord,* Campbell Morgan asks the question, 'Then what is faith?' and answers it by saying:

> 'Faith in God is far more than conviction that He exists. Thousands of people believe in the existence of God, but they have no living faith, no faith like a grain of mustard seed, with the principle of life at its heart. There must be conviction of God, but there must also be a relationship with Him, the going out of the soul towards Him in faith.'

We can perhaps detect echoes here of Christ's parable of the prodigal son who turned homeward to be received with joy by his father. In the language we have been using, faith *that* must be accompanied by faith *in*.

Campbell Morgan adds a third dimension to the nature of faith. He refers to the occasion when the disciples asked Christ to increase their faith, recorded in Luke 17. He says that Christ's answer was intended to tell the disciples they had asked the wrong question. Jesus likened faith to a mustard seed, the smallest of all seeds, which, if planted and nurtured, could grow into a large tree. The disciples had not understood what real faith was, and thought that more would be better. Commenting on the disciples' request and Christ's response, as they still relate to Christians today, Campbell Morgan says,

'The plea is not over. People are still praying for an increase in faith. . . . Our Lord said, "You do not need more faith, but faith of a different kind and nature." It is not a question of quantity, but one of quality. . . . We may define a living faith by saying three things about it. Living faith is, first, conviction concerning the fact of God. It is, secondly, the experience of a relationship with God. Thirdly, and consequently, living faith is absolute submission to the will of God.'

He continues, 'I am emphasising a truth that is fundamental: first, conviction of God; second, relationship with God; and then, obedience to God.' Faith *that*, faith *in*, and faith *to*. Faith *to* is the third dimension. Faith *that* perceives; faith *in* trusts; faith *to* acts.

Faith *that* perceives; faith *in* trusts; faith *to* acts.

It sings, 'I'll go where You want me to go, dear Lord, I'll be what You want me to be.' And suddenly, or gradually, life takes on new meaning. We may legitimately draw the conclusion from 1 Peter 1:3-12 and 2 Peter 1:5-11 that Peter would readily have endorsed all this.

The end of faith

Some years ago now I was invited to give a short epilogue at the end of a youth rally in Birmingham, England. I spoke about 'Heaven's Reservation' from 1 Peter 1:4. I do not remember all

I said that night, but I do remember thinking that the idea of a place reserved in heaven was a very attractive thought. The passage is entitled in the NKJV *'A Heavenly Inheritance'*, in which Peter tells his readers that God, due to His abundant mercy,

'. . . has begotten us again to a living hope through the resurrection of Jesus Christ from the dead, to an inheritance incorruptible and undefiled and that does not fade away, reserved in heaven for you' (1 Peter 1:3, 4).

In verse 21 Peter mentions the post-resurrection glory which was Christ's, suggesting that this is the basis for a believer's hope as he or she anticipates what is to come. He says that God raised Christ from the dead, 'so that your faith and hope are in God'. The prospect of such a future – an invitation to the Marriage Supper of the Lamb with a reserved place at the table – has inspired innumerable thousands ever since it was first written.

We have already looked at 1 Peter 1:3-12, and recall that the relationship between genuine faith and ultimate salvation at the coming of Christ runs through verses 5-10 like a scarlet thread, holding it together and pointing to the last day and 'the glories that would follow' (verse 11). In this short passage of six verses, salvation is mentioned three times and faith (or belief) four times. In verse 9 salvation is said to be 'the end of your faith' – or, as the 1984 edition of the NIV puts it, the 'goal of your faith'. It is incontestable from this passage that salvation, in its fullness, becomes a reality 'at the revelation of Jesus Christ' (verse 7), at the last day, 'at the end of time' as the NEB and GNB translate it (verse 5). Salvation, then, is more than Christ's redeeming death on the cross, and more than what happens when believers first put their faith in Him. It is a process, both in history and in personal experience – a process that will end when Christ comes again and faith is turned into sight. This passage also makes it clear that faith is the means by which salvation is appropriated and personalised from beginning to end.

I have written about this in *A Great Expectation,* an account of the period in English history during the seventeenth century when belief in last-day events, particularly the return of Christ and the interpretation of Daniel and Revelation, was stronger and more widespread in England than at any other time in history. During this period, literally hundreds of books were written and sermons preached by some of the most influential men of the time, including King James I, who published an exposition of the Millennium and spoke openly in the Star Chamber in 1616 of 'the latter dayes drawing on'. Sir Isaac Newton is said to have written more about prophecy than science, including a commentary on Daniel and Revelation written in Latin c. 1670, and published posthumously in English in 1733.

Of the many works from this period I have read, one by John Durant, an independent minister from Canterbury in Kent, illustrates that for centuries Bible students have understood salvation as explained above and outlined in 1 Peter 1:5-8. In his book, *The Salvation of the Saints*, Durant declares: 'Salvation is only yours at the last day.' Salvation had been 'purchased' but not 'completed' at the cross. A believer's salvation was now in hope, as the rightful though suspended inheritance of an heir under age. While accomplished and assured, it was not yet a positive reality, although it was 'as safe as if you had it'. 'Christ keeps the crown 'til the day of His appearance, and in that day He will give it to you.' We are told that Durant's views were similar to those of many other prominent biblical expositors of the time, the renowned Richard Baxter and John Owen, vice-chancellor of Christ Church College, Oxford among them.

> **The prophets of old had diligently searched the Old Testament prophecies concerning this very salvation.**

Ultimate salvation is the end, or the goal, of a living faith.

Peter concludes this remarkable passage by assuring his readers that the prophets of old had diligently searched the Old Testament prophecies concerning this very salvation: the 'sufferings of Christ and the glories that would follow' (verse 11). He concludes by saying that these things had not only been revealed to them, but 'now have been reported to you through those who have preached the gospel to you by the Holy Spirit' (verse 12). It is at that day when the genuineness of their faith will be seen and rewarded. End Time people in every age of history have been people of faith; and, as long as time lasts, they will believe and hope to receive their due reward at the coming of Christ.

The words of Charles Wesley's much-loved hymn, 'Love Divine, All Loves Excelling', capture much of what Peter says in this notable passage (1 Peter 1:5-12), and what has been said by way of explanation as this chapter has developed. As with many hymns, it seems better to be read quietly and thoughtfully as poetry than to be sung lustily in church to the sound of an organ, which often tends to overpower the words:

> *Breathe, O breathe Thy loving Spirit*
> *Into every troubled breast!*
> *Let us all in Thee inherit,*
> *Let us find our promised rest;*
> *Take away our bent to sinning;*
> *Alpha and Omega be;*
> *End of faith, as its beginning,*
> *Set our hearts at liberty.*

> *Finish, then, Thy new creation;*
> *Pure and spotless let us be;*
> *Let us see Thy great salvation*
> *Perfectly restored in Thee;*
> *Changed from glory into glory,*
> *Till in heaven we take our place,*
> *Till we cast our crowns before Thee,*
> *Lost in wonder, love, and praise.*

For reflection and further study

Everybody has faith in someone or something: in a football team, a political leader, technology, a spouse, a vaccine, the pilot of an aeroplane. Consider what it means to have faith in each, and then describe what it means to have faith in Christ.

Compassionate People

11

In his book *The Four Loves*, C. S. Lewis examines the four Greek words for love, which for him represented four types of love. Lewis was regarded as one of the intellectual giants of the twentieth century and one of the most influential writers of his day, never losing the ability to communicate clearly with people of all backgrounds. He wrote more than thirty books, many of them in defence of Christianity at a time when faith had been seriously challenged by World War 2. The Greek words which Lewis examines in *The Four Loves* are *agape* (charity, or unconditional, divine love); *philia* (friendship), or the related *philadelphia* (brotherly love); *storge* (affection); and *eros* (romantic love).

> Love is the defining characteristic of Christianity and must therefore be understood.

Strangely enough, none of these words is translated as 'compassion', which is defined in the dictionary as 'sympathy' or 'pity', and which we usually think of as the practical expression of love, seen in Christ's attitude to the needy and the lost: 'When He saw the multitudes, He was moved with compassion' (Matthew 9:36).

Lewis's book was written from the belief that love is the defining characteristic of Christianity and must therefore be understood – and with the conviction that already in the mid-twentieth century, when the book was published, the word 'love' was overused and insufficiently understood. Few words, in fact, have been devalued in recent times more than 'love'. Then, and even more now, we 'love' everything from children to cars to chocolate to coastal scenery, from our house to our horse or the hibiscus in the garden, from creatures of all kinds to the Creator of them all, and, in obedience to Christ, ourselves and our neighbours. We 'love' them all, and more besides! It seems highly improbable that one word can adequately describe these various 'loves', many of which are not actually love at all in the true sense of the word. It seems almost tantamount to blasphemy to think that the word we would use when referring to affection for our dog or cat could be the same word used to express the love of God for fallen and erring humanity.

> 'By this all will know that you are My disciples, if you have love for one another.'

Only two of the Greek words for love which Lewis discusses are used in the New Testament: *agape* and *philadelphia*, or their derivatives or cognates, as for example in the case of the noun *agape* and the verb *agapao*, 'to love'. The English word 'love' itself appears in twenty-four of the twenty-seven books of the New Testament, mostly translations of *agape* or *agapao*, although *philia* and *philadelphia* are translated as 'love' in eleven New Testament books. Peter mentions love seven times, mostly in his first epistle, and it is what Peter says about love that will claim most of our attention in this chapter. It must be said again, however, that it is difficult, if not impossible, to consider what Peter says in isolation from the rest of the New Testament. The words of Jesus when He declares, 'By this all will know that you are My disciples, if you have love for one another' (John 13:35), and Paul's assertion that, of the three fundamental requirements of Christian belief – faith, hope and love – 'the greatest of these is love' (1 Corinthians 13:13), are cases in point. While Peter's references to love are relatively few compared to the New Testament as a whole, they contain valuable insights that add to our understanding of the necessity and meaning of Christian love.

Loving the unseen Christ
Peter first mentions love in chapter one of his first epistle,

where he reminds the alien pilgrims of Asia Minor of their future heavenly inheritance and the joy this has brought to them despite adversity and persecution. Their salvation will be complete at the revelation of Christ, 'whom having not seen you love' (1 Peter 1:8). The text seems clear enough, but there is more in it than first meets the eye.

> 'Lord, to whom shall we go? You have the words of eternal life.'

There is, for example, the clear implication that there are those who love Christ because they have seen Him. Peter was one of them. He had been with Christ from the very beginning. He was one of the first of four Galilean fishermen whom Jesus had called to leave their nets and follow Him and become fishers of men. For three years or more Peter had been with Jesus, observing His miracles and listening with increasing conviction to His parables. When, well into His ministry, Jesus asked the twelve disciples if they wanted to stay with Him or turn back as some had done, it was Peter who replied, 'Lord, to whom shall we go? You have the words of eternal life' (John 6:68). Peter was one of many who had seen Jesus and heard Him, and had come to love Him enough to follow Him wherever He went.

There may also be the hint of recollections Peter would never forget – his denial of Christ in Pilate's judgement hall, and breakfast by the Sea of Galilee after the resurrection, with the thrice-repeated question Jesus put to Peter in the presence of the other disciples: 'Simon, son of Jonah, do you love Me?' That must have been an embarrassing conversation for Peter. Three times he replied, 'Yes, Lord; You know that I love You.' And then Jesus repeated the invitation He had given Peter at the beginning: 'Follow Me' (John 21:19). Perhaps Jesus, with prophetic insight, was preparing the other disciples for the fact that Peter would soon become their leader in the tumultuous and fast-moving days after Pentecost. His love was now strong again, and his commitment was deep enough to lead the young church through the challenging times of its birth and early growth.

William Barclay says, in commenting on 1 Peter 1:8:

'Peter is drawing an implicit contrast between himself and his readers. It was his great privilege to have known Jesus in the days of His flesh. His readers had not had that joy; but, although they never knew Jesus in the flesh, they love Him.'

To love Christ and to follow Him, despite adversity and persecution, is the essence of early and authentic Christianity, and marks out the pathway to heaven for people of every generation and from all nations. Edmund Clowney also comments on this text and its implications, noting in particular its emphasis on the love of those who have not seen Jesus, yet still love Him:

> 'Peter well knows that it is not his physical association with Jesus that joins him to his Saviour. He knows Jesus as the Son of God by the gift of the Father in heaven. He realises that Gentiles, too, have received the Spirit. By faith we Gentiles who have never seen Jesus may share with Peter in loving Him. It is not necessary for us to have been in Galilee with Jesus. Through the witness of Peter and the other apostles we learn about what Jesus said and did. They bear witness through the Holy Spirit, and by the witness of the Spirit we are brought to know and love the living Lord.'

> **To love Christ and to follow Him, despite adversity and persecution, is the essence of early and authentic Christianity, and marks out the pathway to heaven.**

It is for this love of the unseen Christ that Peter commends the believers who lived in the early years of the Church's history, the original End Time people of the first century. We have remarked more than once, in the previous chapters of this book, that what Peter wrote to the Christians of his day is just as relevant for those who live in the End Time today. We, too, love and serve the Christ we have not seen, looking forward to the day when His promised salvation becomes an eternal reality, the day when we will at last see Him. In Barclay's words, 'If the eye of faith will come when it will be the eye of sight, and we shall see face to face and know even as we are known.'

> **'If the eye of faith endures, the day will come when it will be the eye of sight.'**

The words of a much-loved old hymn could well have been written to affirm the truth and the assurance of Peter's declaration of faith and hope, 'whom having not seen you love':

> *Jesus, these eyes have never seen*
> *That radiant form of Thine;*
> *The veil of sense hangs dark between*
> *Thy blessed face and mine.*
>
> *I see Thee not, I hear Thee not.*
> *Yet art Thou oft with me;*
> *And earth hath ne'er so dear a spot*
> *As when I meet with Thee.*
>
> *Yet, though I have not seen, and still*
> *Must rest in faith alone,*
> *I love Thee, dearest Lord, and will,*
> *Unseen but not unknown.*

The nature of Christian love

Peter's next major reference to love follows in verse 22 of this same chapter, but is not, as can be seen by comparing various versions, in all respects easily translated from the Greek. It is quoted here from the NKJV, together with verse 23 (from which it is inseparable, and which we have previously examined in another context):

> 'Since you have purified your souls in obeying the truth through the Spirit in sincere love of the brethren, love one another fervently with a pure heart, having been born again, not of corruptible seed but incorruptible, through the word of God which lives and abides forever.'

'Love one another fervently with a pure heart, having been born again.'

Perhaps the most significant thing Peter says here is found in the phrase 'sincere love'. It immediately suggests that there is a type of love which is not sincere, just as there is a kind of faith that is not sincere, as we may recall. The marginal alternative for 'sincere' in the NKJV is 'unhypocritical'. Other versions read 'unfeigned love' or 'genuine love', again indicating that love can be feigned or not genuine. Lenski points out that the original reflects an ancient custom in which actors in stage plays wore a mask when representing fictitious characters, and draws the lesson: 'There is always a danger that we pretend like an actor' instead of being genuine. Grudem notes that sincere love 'means love that is genuine, not simply an outward appearance or profession of love'. Insincerity is easily detectable, especially among those who are known to each other, and Peter is speaking particularly of 'sincere love of the brethren'.

> 'He is not satisfied with tolerance or acceptance, far less with formalised distance. He will have love.'

The consequence of insincere love in the lives of believers is that it gives the wrong impression to unbelievers, if not actually being a stumbling block for them. Clowney says, 'Peter therefore exhorts Christians to love one another,' commenting on this passage with necessary clarity:

'Clearly, Peter requires love for fellow Christians as the great mark of true holiness. He is not satisfied with tolerance or acceptance, far less with formalised distance. He will have love, sincere love, without pretence or hypocrisy.'

The second thing of note in 1 Peter 1:22, 23 is that Peter says sincere love is the result of 'having been born again'. Only those who have been born again, regenerate Christians, can know and demonstrate genuine, unfeigned love – not only to fellow believers, it may be said, but also to those who do not yet believe, but who may be watching from a distance and who may be in the valley of decision. The note on 1 Peter 1:22 in the NLT *Life Application Bible* states,

> ' "Sincere love" involves selfless giving; a self-centred person can't truly love.'

' "Sincere love" involves selfless giving; a self-centred person can't truly love. God's love and forgiveness free you to take your eyes off yourselves and to meet others' needs.'

Having defined Christian love as 'sincere love of the brethren' – used here in a gender-inclusive sense – it need not be said that Peter now exhorts them to 'love one another'. Again, this has been made possible because now they are regenerate people, having been born again to a new life with new values and new objectives, enabled 'through the Spirit' and 'through the Word'. The crucial point that must not be overlooked is that the verb here – a derivative of *agapao*, implying a connection with unconditional, divine love – is another imperative, literally 'love ye'. For those who claim to be Christ's, to love one another is not an option. This is not to say that it is always easy, or that it will always be achieved. Those who have been born again are not perfect. They are on a journey together, but have not yet arrived.

Clowney asks the question, 'How can such love be commanded?' and answers by saying:

> 'Peter writes to people divided by the jealousies and hatreds of their past; some were Jews, some Gentiles. To bind them in family love, Peter directs them to the one source. The love that binds the redeemed flows from the love of the Redeemer [i.e. "We love Him because He first loved us" (1 John 4:19)]. Christian love is the love of grace, the love of compassion. For such love to appear, the pride and selfishness of our alienation from God must be swept away. They must be replaced by a heart made new with the motives of grace.'

Lenski is even more frank when he says:

> 'Our loving efforts are not always appreciated, are sometimes received with coolness or even rebuffs. Often, too, brethren are not very lovable, and while we ourselves have love in our heart we do not always manifest it fully.'

Yet the imperative remains, as does the grace by which it can be attempted and achieved.

Brotherly love
Peter speaks of brotherly love in three further texts: each from a different perspective, but all reminding us of the importance of *philadelphia* in the life of the Church as a whole and in the individual believer. Souter defines *philadelphia* as 'love of brothers for each other, hence love of the brethren'. Love between brothers is a unique bond, understood only by those

Compassionate People

who have experienced it. It is affection expressed in comradeship untrammelled by sentimentality or self-interest. It is a form of mateship in which trust and respect are always evident and where deference is always shown for the other. It is therefore a fitting illustration of *philadelphia* as the love that should exist in the Church.

> 'One of the first marks of genuine growth in holiness in individuals and in churches is earnest love for fellow Christians.'

We have already observed the necessity of sincere love in 1 Peter 1:22, where, in the context of the imperative 'love ye', Peter exhorts believers to 'love one another fervently'. Such admonition and the actions and attitudes it generates can best be understood as part of the process of sanctification, the developing life of each born-again Christian enabled by the life-giving power of the Word and the indwelling Spirit. Grudem explains the text, saying:

> 'Once you have begun to grow in holiness so that you now have genuine affection for one another, make your love for each other earnest, deep and strong.... It is a reminder that one of the first marks of genuine growth in holiness in individuals and in churches is earnest love for fellow Christians.'

It is in this context that Peter's further comments on brotherly love can best be understood.

In 1 Peter 2:17, he uses four more imperatives, one of which is 'Love the brotherhood.' The verb in the original comes from *agapao*, 'to love', rather than from *philadelphos*, as might be expected in view of their inherent meanings. The word 'brotherhood' is in fact a derivative of the *philadelphia* family of words, and 'brotherhood' is the only use of this word in the New Testament. By putting together in one short phrase these two most important Greek words for love, Peter indicates just how important brotherly love is in his thinking and in the life of the Church, both as a fulfilment of God's will and as a silent witness to the surrounding pagan society, a culture which Peter puts down to 'the ignorance of foolish men'. Grudem remarks, 'It is a reminder that one of the first marks of genuine growth in holiness in individuals and in churches is earnest love for fellow Christians.'

Francis Schaeffer, one of Christianity's most perceptive and respected apologists in the twentieth century, wrote about the quality and quantity of love in *The Mark of the Christian*, a sequel to *The Church Before the Watching World*:

> **Brotherly love is the distinguishing mark of a true Christian in today's dying culture.**
>
> 'We are to love all Christians "as I", Jesus says, "have loved you". . . . The love He exhibited then and exhibits now is to be our standard. We are to love true Christians as Christ has loved us. . . . The church is to be a loving church in a dying culture. How then is the dying culture going to consider us? . . . He gives the world the right to judge whether you and I are born-again Christians on the basis of our observable love towards all Christians.'

In short, brotherly love is the distinguishing mark of a true Christian in today's dying culture. We may not like it because we feel it finds us falling short, but that's the way it is.

The compelling BBC documentary *RAF at 100* features two brothers, Ewan and Colin McGregor, who fly the earliest planes to have been used in World War I in active combat through to the incredible supersonic Typhoon, with its near-vertical take-off and capacity to break the sound barrier in just a few seconds. The genuine bond between the McGregor brothers is evident at many points in the movie, not least when, with some trepidation, they leave the briefing room for the Typhoon flights, saying goodbye to their mother on the way out to the tarmac. They both fly Typhoons for the first time, under the command of two experienced Typhoon pilots: a fitting climax to their own flying experience, as well as a great finale to the first hundred years of the RAF. The movie has to be seen to be believed, just as brotherly love in the Church has to be seen so that it can be believed.

Peter's next reference to brotherly love is in 1 Peter 3:8: 'Finally, all of you be of one mind, having compassion for one another; love as brothers, be tenderhearted, be courteous.' This is Peter's only use of the word 'compassion', and is one of the few texts in the New Testament outside the gospels which uses the word. Barclay says categorically, 'There can be no Christianity without compassion.' This text also uses the Greek word *sumpatheis,* from which we get the English 'sympathy'. Compassion is sympathy in action. As already noted, Christ's ministry was undergirded by compassion. Mark's record of another instance says that Jesus was moved with compassion for the multitudes, 'because they were like sheep not having a shepherd' (Mark 6:34). Today it might be said that He would have seen the multitudes and had compassion on them, for they were refugees, having lost everything, driven from their homes by war, hunger and persecution.

Commenting on this text, Clowney reminds us of Christ's parable of the good Samaritan who 'showed a love that could not be demanded, the love of mercy. He made himself a neighbour in the love of compassion.' He then makes the application:

'We have received the free compassion of Christ's grace. ... The love that He now requires of us His people is not a self-righteous, legalistic love, working to score points for heaven. Rather, as those who are heirs of the blessing of life eternal, we must model our love on the love of God in Christ. God's compassion demands love like His, the love of free grace. Only God's love, poured out into our hearts by the Holy Spirit, can move us to show His compassion.'

> 'There can be no Christianity without compassion.'

It is hard to disagree with that.

A wider love

Most of Peter's exhortations to love refer to brotherly love or 'love of the brethren'. His only specific reference to a love which includes all people – like that of God Himself, which is unconditional and knows no boundaries – appears in 2 Peter 1:7: '[Add] to godliness brotherly kindness, and to brotherly kindness love.' It is his final admonition in the 'Ladder of Faith', which we considered in chapter nine, and is the last virtue which precedes the promise that those who do such things will find an abundant entrance to God's kingdom.

That Peter's reference to love in this text applies to a wider love appears from the fact that two different Greek words are used in the original, *philadelphia* and *agape*: the former always restricted to brotherly love, and the latter having the wider connotation of love for all. Furthermore, it would be superfluous to add 'love' to 'brotherly love' as another virtue if they meant the same thing or something very similar. Lenski, with his keen perception of differences in the meaning of New Testament Greek words, says here, 'We may say that this final item, "love", is broader than brotherly love, and that it extends to all men, as does the *agape* love of God.' Barclay's comment is likewise unambiguous:

> 'The ladder of Christian virtue must end in Christian love. Not even affection for the brethren is enough; the Christian must end with a love which is as wide as that love of God which causes His sun to rise on the just and on the unjust, and sends His rain on the evil and the good. The Christian must show to all men the love which God has shown to him.'

To love those whose foibles and failings are known to us is, it must be admitted, harder than to love those whom we have never seen. When Peter described the ladder of virtues which reaches up to heaven, he affirmed that both are necessary. *Christians are to show compassion to all people, regardless of their age, gender, ethnicity, culture, education, status or religion.* The reason is simple:

> *In Christ there is no east nor west,*
> *In Him no south or north;*
> *But one great fellowship of love*
> *Throughout the whole wide earth.*

If that seems an unattainable impossibility, as very often it does, let it at least be kept before us as the hallmark of authentic Christian being and living.

For reflection and further study

'Since you have purified yourselves in obeying the truth through the Spirit in sincere love of the brethren, love one another fervently with a pure heart' (1 Peter 1:22). Civil society expects us to be 'tolerant' of others who are different from us. Explain the difference between 'tolerance' of another person and 'love' for one another, as understood by Peter.

12 Distinctive People

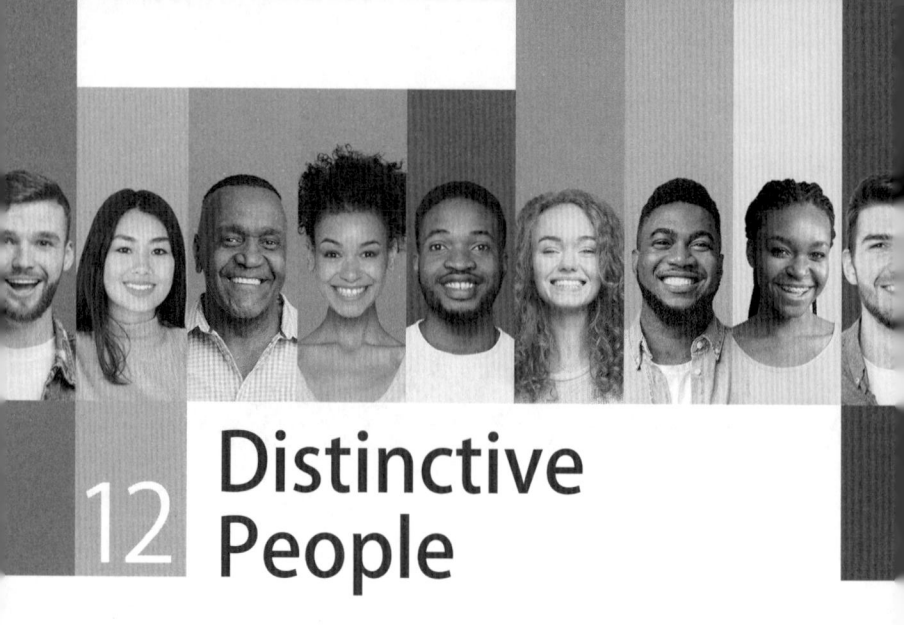

In the nineteenth century there was a small religious sect, mainly in the English county of Essex, who called themselves 'The Peculiar People', taking their name from the KJV translation of 1 Peter 2:9: 'But ye are . . . a peculiar people.' They practised faith healing, rejected medical help (which sometimes led to death), and were strict observers of the Lord's day, in some places having four services on Sunday. Some of the women are said to have worn black bonnets to distinguish them from others, even those of the same faith. Needless to say, The Peculiar People were a passing phenomenon, soon consigned to history. They do, however, provide an interesting introduction to what Peter says about being distinctive.

This chapter is the logical continuation of chapter eleven, which addressed the theme of love and compassion, having cited C. S. Lewis (the most effective Christian apologist in the second half of the twentieth century) and Francis Schaeffer (founder of the L'Abri Fellowship in Switzerland and a leading Christian philosopher whose collected works fill five large volumes). Lewis believed that love is the defining characteristic of authentic Christianity, and Schaeffer maintained that 'The church is to be a loving church in a dying culture,' claiming that the evidence Christians have been born again is 'observable love'. Christians sometimes talk about 'distinctive beliefs', some special doctrines or truths they hold dear and which they believe set them apart from others, including other Christians. Here is a salutary reminder that being distinctive

> **Being distinctive is determined not by what we believe or by what we do, but by who we are.**

is determined not by what we believe or by what we do, but by who we are; and we are much indebted to Lewis and Schaeffer for reminding us that love lies at the heart of Christian distinctiveness.

Neither Peter nor any of the other New Testament writers use the words 'distinctive' or 'distinctiveness'. Nor does the original use any word which can be translated as 'special', which appears only in the NKJV, but not in any other more recent translations. They all use the phrase 'God's own people', as in the NRSV, or words which convey a similar meaning. The NRSV of 1 Peter 2:9 reads,

'But you are a chosen race, a royal priesthood, a holy nation, God's own people, in order that you may proclaim the mighty acts of him who called you out of darkness into his marvelous light.'

There is in fact scant support in the original Greek for the use of 'special' or 'peculiar' in any translation. To belong to God and to be one of His own is indeed special, but not in a way that makes us feel better than others. This is not to say that what we believe and what we do are of no consequence whatsoever, as we see when we read what Peter says. It is, however, to say that we must never lose sight of what is basic, and that we must not be led astray into believing that anything we do or think earns us Brownie points on our way to the kingdom.

Lifestyle

We are not yet ready to leave 1 Peter 2:9, which can only be fully understood in the light of what follows. Verses 11 and 12 are crucial in this respect, for they introduce two key themes which flow on through the rest of the epistle – Christian conduct and Christian influence. Under the NKJV sub-heading for this passage, 'Living Before the World', Peter says:

> 'Beloved, I beg you as sojourners and pilgrims, abstain from fleshly lusts which war against the soul, having your conduct honorable among the Gentiles, that when they speak against you as evildoers, they may, by your good works which they observe, glorify God in the day of visitation.'

Commenting on these texts, Barclay declares that the Christian's life must be so evidently good that the slanders of heathen enemies 'may be demonstrated to be false', and says:

> 'Here is timeless truth. Whether we like it or not, every Christian is an advertisement for Christianity; by his life he either commends it to others or makes them think less of it. The strongest missionary force in the world is a Christian life.'

> **The Christian's life must be so evidently good that the slanders of heathen enemies 'may be demonstrated to be false'.**

He goes on to point out that in Peter's day there were many slanderous and false accusations made about Christians, which throws light on verse 12. They were accused, among other things, of cannibalism, immorality, incest; of turning slaves against their masters; and, perhaps most damaging of all, of disloyalty to Caesar. Peter's argument is that the only way for Christians to refute these false and damaging misrepresentations was to live in such a way that their behaviour demonstrated that the accusations were unfounded.

Verse 9 also indicates that the Christian Church had replaced Israel as the channel through which God could speak to the world. This new 'royal priesthood' and 'holy nation', the Church, was to bear witness to His grace and mercy, as it had been intended that God's people in Old Testament times were to do. The Church was God's plan B. It is perhaps difficult for some to grasp just what that meant. In Peter's day, there was no such thing as evangelism in the sense that we have come to know it. There were no public meetings at which to explain what Christians believed or why they believed it. Even to have attempted it would have brought down upon them the wrath of the Roman authorities like the proverbial ton of bricks. Peter is saying that the only way to bear witness to the world is by an appropriate lifestyle commensurate with basic Christian belief, an assertion that we will consider more fully in a later chapter. The point here is that the Church and every believer were to be lights shining in a very dark place. Schaeffer recognised that an authentic Christian lifestyle is as necessary today as it was in the first century, perhaps even more so, and made the point with characteristic frankness:

> **'If you practise untruth while talking about truth, the real thinkers will just say, "Garbage."'**

'Our credibility is already minus 5 if we do not say what is false and wrong in contrast to what is true and right. It is minus 405 if we are not willing to stand practically in the area of antithesis. . . . We must practise the truth even when it is costly. . . . If you think that those who have rejected the plastic culture and are sick of hypocrisy are going to be impressed when you talk about truth and at the same time practise untruth, you are wrong. They will never listen. You have cut the ground from under yourself. We live in a generation that does not believe that such a thing as truth is possible, and if you practise untruth while talking about truth, the real thinkers will just say, "Garbage." '

This, if we are not mistaken, is precisely what Peter was saying in the language of his day. That it is equally as relevant now is equally clear to those who have eyes to see and ears to hear.

Holiness and godliness
One of the most challenging dimensions of a Christian lifestyle is Peter's consistent emphasis on holiness and godliness – a recurring theme we have previously noted. It appears first in 1 Peter 1:15: 'But as he who called you is holy, you also be holy in all your conduct.' The Greek word for 'holy', used twice here, is *hagios,* which means 'separate' or 'set apart'. Godliness is mentioned at the beginning of Peter's second epistle, where he states that God 'has given us everything we need for a godly

life' (1:3, NIV) as 'partakers of the divine nature, having escaped the corruption that is in the world through lust' (2 Peter 1:4). This second epistle ends on a similar note, with the question, 'What kind of people ought you to be?' and the answer, 'You ought to live holy and godly lives' (3:11, NIV), looking forward to Christ's return. Holiness and godliness seem out of reach for most of us, as they would have seemed to believers in Peter's day. Yet we may take some comfort from the fact that *hagios* means 'separate' or 'set apart', and not perfect; and that godliness comes from a Greek word that means 'piety' or 'God-fearing', and not 'without sin'. Nevertheless, the standard is high, and it means that Christians are called to a lifestyle that is different from that of those who are not believers. Such a lifestyle distinguishes them.

The new life of a Christian is also different from the life it used to be. Commenting on 1 Peter 1:14, Grudem notes the strong contrast between a Christian lifestyle and behaviour that conforms 'to the passions of your former ignorance'. Without arguing for perfection, he explains,

'The idea of holiness for God's people includes not simply a concept of separation in general, but a specifically moral sense of separation from evil and dedication to a life of righteousness.... To be holy 'as God is holy' includes a full and pervading holiness that reaches to every aspect of our personalities. It involves not only avoiding outward sin, but also maintaining an instinctive delight in God and His holiness as an undercurrent of heart and mind throughout the day.'

Barclay points out that the root meaning of *hagios* is 'different'. He says the Temple in Jerusalem was holy because it was different; that the Sabbath is holy because it is different from other days in the week; and that Christians are different from other men and women – not, as already noted, perfect, but because they are 'set apart', and therefore distinctive.

In a chapter entitled 'Grace and the Sanctified Life' in his book *Redeeming Grace,* Harry Lowe refers to Romans 7 and Paul's despairing cry, 'O wretched man that I am!' (Verse 24.) As many Bible students have noted, this was the cry of a converted Christian about the intensity of the spiritual struggle he faced after conversion. Lowe points out that the Christian 'lives in two worlds simultaneously', meaning that after conversion he has two natures, each pulling in a different direction, adding:

> 'So long as this is so, he lives in a state of tension. Temporarily he lives in this world; as a man of flesh and blood he is subject to the conditions of mortal life; he is a "son of Adam", like all his fellow men, and with them he is subject to the law that "in Adam all die". Spiritually, however, he has passed from death to life, from the realm of darkness to the kingdom of light . . . he has been raised "to walk in newness of life", a citizen of the new world, a member of the new creation, no longer "in Adam" but "in Christ".'

> **Christians, while not perfect, are nevertheless different and therefore distinctive.**

The fact that Peter enjoins believers to '[lay] aside all malice, all deceit, hypocrisy, envy, and all evil speaking', begging them to 'abstain from fleshly lusts', shows that he too recognises the struggles of those who have been born again (1 Peter 1:23 and 2:1, 11). The truth is that Christians, while not perfect, are nevertheless different and therefore distinctive.

Humility and submissiveness
Humility is a virtue that shows itself in submissiveness, a word for which there are many synonyms, including 'unresisting', 'yielding', 'unassertive', 'amenable' and 'compliant'. The verb 'to submit' means 'to give way' or 'to surrender oneself'. Peter has much to say about being humble and submissive, especially in his first epistle, and it is quite apparent from his comments that humility and submissiveness are very important characteristics of the Christian life. Before we consider what Peter says, however, it may be helpful to recall the New Testament context of Peter's letters.

The outstanding example of humility in the New Testament is that of Christ Himself, recorded by Paul in Philippians chapter two. Frequently thought of as the classic New Testament statement about the nature of Christ, it is in fact a statement about the true nature of humility. That is clear from verse 3: 'Let nothing be done through selfish ambition or conceit, but in lowliness of mind let each esteem others better than himself.' Conceit is pride, the antithesis of humility, so Paul goes on to say, 'Let this mind be in you which was also in Christ Jesus' (verse 5). In other words, Christ's attitude is the pattern for all believers. Then follows the account of Christ's condescension. Paul says that Christ, who was God, 'made himself nothing' and 'humbled himself by becoming obedient to death – even death on a cross' – the death that was reserved for criminals and the lowest of the low (Philippians 2:7, 8, NIV).

> 'Be submissive to one another, and be clothed with humility. . . . Humble yourselves under the mighty hand of God.'

We do not know if Peter had seen or heard these words, although it is possible that he had, since Philippians was written c. AD 55-57, some six or seven years before Peter wrote his first epistle. Whether or not he knew what Paul had written, Peter speaks at length, strongly and unmistakably, about humility and submissiveness being essential marks of authentic Christianity. In a sequence of settings from 1 Peter 2:13 through to 5:5 he enjoins:

- Submission to government as the will of God (1 Peter 2:13-15)
- Submission of servants (slaves) to their masters, as this is commendable to God (1 Peter 2:18-25)
- Submission of spouses to each other (1 Peter 3:1-7)
- Submission of younger people to their elders (1 Peter 5:5)

He then concludes by saying, 'Yes, all of you be submissive to one another, and be clothed with humility. . . . Humble yourselves under the mighty hand of God' (1 Peter 5:5, 6). It is not possible to know how those in the first century who read these specific and direct exhortations reacted, but if it was anything like the reactions we might see today, they would have stood aghast at the seeming impossibility of compliance. Humility does not come easily or naturally, and it would have seemed as though they were being asked to climb a steep mountain without any practice.

Commenting on verse 5, Grudem speaks of 'the atmosphere of humility towards one another which should characterise relationships among Christians' and says:

'No one is exempt, for Peter includes church officers and non-officers, young and old, new Christians and mature believers. . . . The term "humility" speaks of an attitude which puts others first, which thinks of the desires, needs, and ideas of others as more worthy of attention than one's own.'

> Christ is the supreme example of obedience, and of that submission which made Him 'obedient unto death'.

Many a pastor will know from experience what he is talking about! As Clowney affirms, 'Mutual submission is the key to the pattern of life in Christ's church.'

Humility in general is certainly not a sign of the times, but it should be a sign of God's End Time people. Alan Richardson, a contributor to and editor of *A Theological Word Book of the Bible*, says in his article on pride that the 'biblical teaching about pride, and its converse, humility, . . . is unparalleled in other religions and ethical systems'. Peter's strong teaching on the subject is, of course, included in this comment. Richardson adds that Christ, by His words, and even more by His life and deeds, 'introduced a new virtue – Christian humility – into the world'. It makes such humility truly distinctive.

Obedience and disobedience

Both these words imply the existence of someone or some higher power with the authority to require compliance to prescribed rules and regulations. In the case of Christianity, God is the higher power, and it is to Him that Christians are ultimately accountable. One writer notes: 'To obey is to conform, in humility, to that which God prescribes.' Another says, 'Obedience lies at the heart of Christian existence.' Again, Christ is the supreme example of obedience, and of that submission which made Him 'obedient unto death', and through whose obedience salvation becomes possible: 'For as by one man's disobedience many were made sinners, so also by one Man's obedience many will be made righteous' (Romans 5:19).

> 'I will put My law in their minds, and write it on their hearts.'

Peter speaks of both obedience and disobedience, using Greek words which mean, respectively, 'to hearken submissively' and 'to be unpersuaded'. He refers to obedience three times in 1 Peter 1: again, an indication of the importance Peter attaches to it, and of his desire that his readers will recognise the need to comply as they proceed along the way to the kingdom. In each of these three references Peter comments on obedience from a different perspective.

At the beginning of the first epistle, he reminds believers that they have been 'chosen according to the foreknowledge of God the Father, through the sanctifying work of the Spirit, to be obedient to Jesus Christ' (1 Peter 1:2, NIV). Christian obedience does not come about by strenuous and regular personal effort. It is the 'sanctifying work of the Spirit' which enables acceptable obedience, as has been pointed out in previous chapters. It is an ever-timely reminder that obedience comes from a regenerate heart, and perhaps of the new-covenant promise made by God: 'I will put My law in their minds, and write it on their hearts' (Jeremiah 31:33). Jeremiah wrote that a day is coming when God's law will no longer be inscribed only on tables of stone, but on the fleshy tables of the 'heart', imparting a desire to obey – the obedience of love and gratitude. Grudem speaks of 'the daily obedience of believers', and thinks that Peter's readers realised that their obedience was always incomplete, 'that even the most mature Christians were painfully aware of remaining sin, and that God's purpose, "obedience to Jesus Christ", would never be completely fulfilled in this life'.

This is a further reminder that obedience does not lead to perfection. Samuel Chadwick, a Methodist minister and a former president of the Wesleyan Methodist Conference, wrote in his book, *The Call to Christian Perfection*, of the impossibility of extreme perfectionism:

'Christian perfection has been regarded as claiming not only deliverance from sin, but from all error, limitation and defect. Such is manifestly impossible. Christian perfection is not infallibility. It does not deify men. It does not dehumanise humanity; it sanctifies it. A clean heart does not imply a perfect head. So long as we are in this world, there will be unavoidable errors and imperfections of judgement.'

Secondly, in 1 Peter 1:14, Peter refers to 'obedient children', perhaps an allusion to familial obedience: that of a trusting child to a beloved father, as is the human relationship to God, and an attitude easily understood from normal family life.

Peter's final reference to obedience in this first chapter is in verse 22, where he speaks of 'obeying the truth': again, a reality made possible by the fact that true believers have been 'born again' (verse 23). 'Truth' is a concept that is well known to End Time people today, often in the sense of cognitive assent to certain doctrines ('propositional truth', as it is sometimes called). While this is entirely appropriate, even necessary, it must not be thought of as the entirety of biblical truth, as Grudem points out in his comments on this text: ' "The truth" here carries a sense of the true way pleasing to God, including not merely the Gospel message, but the whole of Christian teaching on doctrine and life.' The key emphasis in this text is, of course, the same as that in the previous texts – the necessity of obedience as a defining characteristic of authentic Christianity.

> 'What will be the end of those who do not obey the gospel of God?'

We have concentrated on the major texts in which Peter enjoins obedience, for lack of space passing over most of those where he refers to disobedience. His scathing denunciation of the false teachers who have wrought havoc in the church (2 Peter 2) describes a betrayal of the true Christian lifestyle and a classic example of how Christians should not live. They have forsaken 'the right way' and turned 'from the holy commandment delivered to them' (verses 15, 21). We should note in conclusion the uncomfortable question Peter asks: 'What will be the end of those who do not obey the gospel of God?' (1 Peter 4:17.)

While we know the answer to this searching question, it is never amiss to be reminded that judgement is coming, and that it begins 'at the house of God'. At the same time, we should not overlook Peter's reference to 'the gospel', which is always the catalyst for true Christian obedience. In the final analysis, hope prevails and the good news triumphs over the bad. God's salvation, available to all who believe, will ensure that those who believe are spared the inevitable and just fate of those who do not.

We set out at the beginning of this chapter to discover what Peter says about Christian distinctiveness. Continuing from chapter eleven, it is clear that Peter believes that what makes Christians truly distinctive is lifestyle, rather than any confession of faith. The lifestyle he advocates begins with love, proceeds with holiness and godliness, continues with humility and submissiveness, and concludes with obedience. It is a lifestyle in stark contrast to the Roman culture of Peter's day, and to the prevailing pagan culture of our time. Peter's emphases, put together, describe well what a distinctive Christian lifestyle really is, and why it shines so brightly in the darkness of paganism and secularism.

Many of my early years in school were spent in the English town of Bedford, where John Bunyan spent twelve years in prison for being different from the established Church of the time, and where he wrote *Pilgrim's Progress,* that all-time classic allegory of the Christian life. Bunyan's hymn, 'He Who Would Valiant Be', was the school song which we often sang in assembly, and I can still remember the feelings of determination and anticipation I felt every time we sang it. The truth is, as Bunyan says, that being a Christian requires us to follow Christ constantly, wherever He may lead us, and with the help of the Spirit to live an obedient life, however difficult it seems and however different it may make us feel, until we reach the celestial city.

He who would valiant be, 'gainst all disaster,
Let him in constancy follow the Master.
There's no discouragement shall make him once relent
His first avowed intent to be a pilgrim.

Distinctive People

> *Who so beset him round with dismal stories*
> *Do but themselves confound; his strength the more is.*
> *No foes shall stay his might, though he with giants fight;*
> *He will make good his right to be a pilgrim.*
>
> *Since, Lord, thou dost defend us with Thy Spirit,*
> *We know we at the end shall life inherit.*
> *Then, fancies, flee away! I'll fear not what men say;*
> *I'll labour night and day to be a pilgrim.*

For reflection and further study

Christians are often seen as distinctive because of what they believe and the lifestyle practices they adopt – for example, keeping the Sabbath holy. But 'being distinctive is determined not by what we believe or by what we do, but by who we are' (page 133). Why?

13 | Steadfast People

The *Reader's Digest Oxford Complete Wordfinder* gives twenty-eight synonyms for the word 'steadfast', including 'resolute', 'unwavering', 'unflinching', 'determined' and 'unfaltering'. The word 'steadfast' itself has a long history in the English language, deriving from the Old English word *stedefaest*, dating from the Middle Ages. The same is true of the related noun 'steadfastness', meaning perseverance or doggedness. Peter uses both 'steadfast' and 'steadfastness', and the synonyms cited above help us to understand more clearly what he means. Both words can only correctly be used of people who have faced difficulties or hardship, been through trials and temptations, or experienced suffering or persecution, and who have made a conscious decision to pursue the light at the end of the tunnel and to take what comes, whatever it may be and however long it might last. Such people are truly steadfast, and there have been more of them through history than could be counted – many of them in Peter's day and in the years that followed under successive Roman emperors. Peter has 'steadfast' and 'steadfastness' in mind when speaking specifically of two major threats: suffering and persecution, and the devil, who pursues God's people

> Such people are truly steadfast, and there have been more of them through history than could be counted.

144

relentlessly like a lion, seeking whom he may destroy.

While Peter uses these words sparingly, each on one occasion only, the tone of 1 Peter is, throughout, one of encouragement to persevere and remain resolute in times of trial and persecution. The first chapter of 1 Peter begins by reminding readers of the 'living hope' that comes from looking forward to the future revelation of Christ, and the 'incorruptible' heavenly inheritance that will be theirs in that day. They are called to 'glory', he assures them, and will receive an abundant entrance into the heavenly kingdom. They can rejoice 'with joy inexpressible' when thinking of what lies ahead (1 Peter 1:3-9). Further, they are 'chosen by God and precious', 'a holy nation' (1 Peter 2:4, 9). Peter intends that these reminders of the joy that lies ahead and their present status in God's eyes will sustain his readers and help them to keep focused on who they are and what is to come beyond the trials and difficulties of the present (which, in any case, are only 'for a little while'). In the introduction to his commentary on First Peter, Wayne Grudem explains:

> 'The purpose of 1 Peter is to encourage readers to grow in their trust in God and their obedience to Him throughout their lives, but especially when they suffer.'

The full intent of Peter's first epistle, however, and the background to his call to steadfastness can only be understood completely within the historical context in which it was written.

The historical background
As noted above, it is clear from a careful reading of this epistle that 1 Peter was written against a background of present and future suffering to encourage early Christians who faced tribulation and persecution. Surprisingly, perhaps, Peter does not use the word 'persecution', instead using the word 'suffering' throughout the epistle. The word appears eight times when referring to the physical suffering of his readers and to the sufferings of Christ. In the same vein, and of equal significance, verses six and seven of chapter one speak of believers having already been 'grieved' or 'distressed' by 'various trials', or by 'all kinds of trials' as the NIV puts it, and

of a faith that is 'tested by fire'. The literal reality of these comments will become clearer shortly, as will also their lasting relevance to Christians in every age and land and from every background.

> 'First Peter was written to meet no theological heresy; it was written to strengthen men and women in jeopardy of their lives.'

Some commentators have made light of the suffering mentioned by Peter in this epistle, concentrating instead on the joy and the blessings of the future salvation to be revealed at Christ's coming, and claiming that suffering was not universally experienced in the early church and that it was only sporadic. The text of 1 Peter does not support such views, as we shall see. In fact, it only makes complete sense when considered from the opposite point of view. Barclay says, 'First Peter was written to meet no theological heresy; it was written to strengthen men and women in jeopardy of their lives.'

In order for this to be clear, it is necessary to know just when and why 1 Peter was written in the first place, and when and how the persecution it refers to arose. Grudem says that AD 64 is 'more fully attested by historical data' than any other possible date. A note in the introduction to 1 Peter in the ESV states: 'Peter wrote this letter in the mid-60s AD.' A similar note in the NLT also dates the epistle at 64, and says it was written at a time of 'great persecution at the hands of the Emperor Nero'. Lenski begins the introduction to his commentary on 1 Peter by saying, 'The first epistle of St Peter was written by the apostle while he was in Rome not long before his death under Nero in the year 64.' Barclay, who gives an extensive introduction to his commentary on 1 Peter, states that this letter was written from Rome 'in the days immediately following the first persecution of the Christians by Nero', although he gives a date after 64. It seems clear enough that the earliest date for 1 Peter is AD 64, and that it was occasioned by the persecution initiated by the Roman Emperor Nero.

When and how Nero's persecution took place is also an important aspect of the historical background to 1 Peter. In July AD 64, a great fire broke out in Rome. It burned for six days and nights before being brought under control, and then broke out again. Two thirds of the city was destroyed. It was rumoured that Nero himself had started the fire so that Rome could be rebuilt according to his wishes. Aware of the rumours, and wanting to remove suspicion from himself, Nero accused the Christians in Rome of starting the fire, and the persecution began. It is highly improbable that Christians were responsible, for even if they had thought of it – an unlikely possibility – they would have known that it would bring down the wrath of Nero upon them, along with the destruction of many houses and great loss of life. The Roman historian Tacitus recorded that an *ingens multitudo,* a huge multitude, of Christians perished, and it is most likely that Peter was among them as the persecution intensified. One historian has described Nero as 'one of the most infamous men who ever lived'. Any man who could kill his own mother or his wife on his way to the top because they thwarted his ambitions deserves such an epithet. Nero killed both – his mother Agrippina and his wife Octavia – and he is said to have disposed of his mistress Poppaea, as well. He is arguably the most notorious and brutal psychopath in history. The persecution of Christians continued spasmodically for the next three centuries, but at few times was it more severe than under Nero in the first century.

Such is the historical context in which Peter's first epistle was written and in which he lived out the last few months of his life. Although many of the details are not recorded, the evidence indicates AD 64 as the year in which he died, a date supported by most writers excepting a few who give various dates between 65 and 68. Peter would not have been human if he had faced this short future without any apprehension. He would almost certainly have remembered Jesus' last words to him by the sea of Galilee after the resurrection:

> 'Most assuredly, I say to you, when you were younger, you girded yourself and walked where you wished; but when you are old, you will stretch out your hands, and another will gird you and carry you where you do not wish' (John 21:18).

John then adds, 'This He spoke, signifying by what death he would glorify God.' According to tradition Peter was crucified upside down in the Circus Maximus in Rome, led out to his death perhaps from the Mamertine Prison, where it is believed he spent his last days.

Steadfast in suffering and persecution

> Because Christ is their example in suffering, they 'were called' to suffer as He did.

Peter mentions suffering in every chapter of his first epistle. Clearly, it figures prominently in his thinking, and confirms what has been said previously about 1 Peter having been written against a background of various trials and persecution. He tells his readers in chapter two that, because Christ is their example in suffering, they 'were called' to suffer as He did (1 Peter 2:20, 21). We may be sure that this would have been of some comfort to those who read this epistle and who themselves suffered for Christ's sake. Commenting on this passage, Clowney remarks, 'We take up our cross to follow Him. He has left us an example, a pattern to follow.' It is easy enough to say or to read, but never easy to put into practice.

Some of Peter's references to suffering relate to suffering in general, which comes to all Christians at some time or another – perhaps as a result of chronic illness or an accident or war, or even the mental suffering that comes from being rejected or insulted. Verse 19 relates to the suffering of slaves 'wrongfully' inflicted by harsh masters, but in the following verses the context makes it clear that Peter refers to the physical suffering Christ endured at Calvary. Verses 22-25 contain many references to Isaiah 53; the word 'stripes' in the NKJV translation of verse 24 is elsewhere translated 'wounds' (NIV). In the phrase 'when He suffered' (verse 23), Peter uses a form of the Greek verb *pascho,* meaning 'to suffer or endure'. This word is used throughout the New Testament, particularly when referring to the sufferings of Christ, the 'Paschal Lamb'.

The key passage on suffering, 1 Peter 4:12-19, begins with the injunction: 'Beloved, do not think it strange concerning the fiery trial which is to try you.' While some modern translations suggest that the trials have already begun, Lenski explains that the original indicates they are still to come. Lenski's great strength is his detailed knowledge of the Greek, and it is nowhere demonstrated more clearly than here. He explains that the imperatives and indicatives and participles in the original 'lead us to believe that Peter is no longer speaking of sufferings such as his readers had already experienced . . . but of impending sufferings that would be far more severe'. These sufferings are already 'on the way', and 'the worst is to be expected' because Nero and the imperial government in Rome are now hostile to Christianity, 'treating it as a *religio illicita,* a forbidden religion'. Lenski also notes that the 'fiery trial' which is coming is really a 'fiery ordeal', *purosis* in the Greek, a 'burning': none of the trials which Christians had suffered so far deserved this description. Further, verse 16 refers specifically to those who will suffer 'as a Christian', Lenski again commenting, 'The implication is that if any one of the readers suffers as a murderer, etc., this is not suffering as a Christian. Such a reader would suffer as the criminal he would really be.' Peter means what he says in this text: that the suffering arising from this persecution is suffering endured by Christians for their faith.

This entire passage, 1 Peter 4:12-19, calls for careful reading and reflection since it presents, among other things, three key facts which summarise the essence of Peter's concern:

> **If any one of the readers suffers as a murderer, etc., this is not suffering as a Christian.**

- Suffering and persecution are inevitable.
- The 'fiery trial', or 'ordeal' (NRSV), is still to come.
- Some will suffer specifically because they are Christians.

All this is precisely what happened in the Roman summer of AD 64 and beyond, under the persecutions instigated by Nero. Tacitus described it in his *Annals*: 'Covered with the skins of beasts, they were torn apart by dogs and perished, or were nailed to crosses, or were doomed to the flames and burned to serve as nightly illumination when daylight had expired' – human torches, in fact. Others have also recorded these events, and it is known that the Circus Maximus in Rome was the venue for the public viewing of these atrocities. Another historian, Sulpicius Severus, later told the same terrible story in his *Chronicles:*

> 'Even new kinds of death were invented so that, being in the skins of wild beasts, they perished by being devoured by dogs, while many were crucified, or slain by fire, and not a few were set apart for this purpose, that when the day came to a close, they should be consumed to serve for light during the night.'

Peter was one of those who suffered, and he saw suffering as something that could be expected, to be regarded as participation in Christ's sufferings. It was therefore a reason for rejoicing, looking forward to the day when Christ's glory would be revealed. Such advice led to the willing martyrdom of thousands in AD 64 and in the years that followed, and to untold millions who through the ages have suffered for the 'crime' of being Christians. It is not amiss to note that in some parts of the world Christians are today still suffering for the same 'crime'.

Steadfast against the enemy

Peter's most challenging call to steadfastness, 1 Peter 5:8, 9, begins with two imperatives: 'Be sober' and 'Be vigilant'. These imperatives confirm that there are no options here. If Peter's readers do not accept his advice, the consequences will be dire indeed. The necessity for vigilance is emphasised in the next phrase: 'Because your adversary the devil walks about like a roaring lion, seeking whom he may devour.' Peter seems to take it for granted that his readers know who and what he is talking about. The devil was from of old, from before the beginning. He had been cast out of heaven before the world began (Rev. 12:9); Jesus said that He had seen Satan fall from heaven (Luke 10:18); and Peter – who, as noted previously, was conversant with Paul's epistles – would most likely have known that Paul had urged the Ephesians, 'Stand against the wiles of the devil' (Ephesians 6:11).

During the final months of World War 2, I lived with my parents and siblings in an old farmhouse some fifty miles north-east of London. I was ten at the time. These were the days when Hitler was making a last, desperate attempt to destroy London, using the V1 and V2 rockets, pilotless aircraft packed with high explosives, with engines programmed to cut out when over the target. Occasionally there were errors in timing or routing. I recall one night, when the air-raid siren had sounded the imminent arrival of enemy aircraft, hearing one of these missiles flying in our direction. Suddenly the engine cut out. We waited with bated breath for what seemed like an eternity. It was in fact only a minute, but it was the longest minute in my life. Then we heard the explosion. In the morning, we saw a huge crater in a field about half a mile from the house. It taught me a valuable lesson I still remember. The enemy was real, even though he could not be seen, and his objective in those last days of the war was clear – to destroy London, or as much of it as possible.

> It was in fact only a minute, but it was the longest minute in my life. Then we heard the explosion.

The enemy Peter is talking about is also on a mission of destruction – to destroy Christ, the Church and every believer. Peter uses the word 'devour', translated from the Greek *katapino*, literally meaning 'to swallow up', 'to gobble', or 'to gulp down': very appropriate to the intention of the 'roaring lion' who seeks to devour his prey. The vivid images these words conjure up make it impossible to miss the point Peter is making to the End Time people in his day. The enemy is alive and abroad. He may be unseen, but his objective is still the same, and you are the target: therefore, be vigilant. End Time people living today should take note!

> He may be unseen, but his objective is still the same, and you are the target: therefore, be vigilant.

He is, moreover, a cunning, wily, scheming foe, as Paul had warned the Ephesians. It was advice that applied not only to those at Ephesus, but to Christians everywhere who were aware that they were engaged in a spiritual conflict with a very real enemy, as indeed we still are. Christians today, however, find themselves in a different situation, when the enemy's strategies have changed and belief in the reality of the devil has all but disappeared. The first verse of a frequently quoted poem underlines this reality:

> *Men don't believe in a devil now,*
> *as their fathers used to do;*
> *They reject one creed because it's old,*
> *another because it's new.*

Commenting on today's 'general disbelief in the devil', Clowney says that Satan 'could not ask for better cover than the illusion that he does not exist'. Anyone who has been influenced by this delusion has been taken for a very long ride that will ultimately end in disaster.

Some have seen Peter's description of the devil as a 'roaring lion' as merely metaphorical, but the archaeological evidence tells a different story. The lion was a well-known animal in the first-century Roman Empire, and the punishment of *damnatio ad bestia*, 'condemnation by beasts', had been known across the empire since the third century BC. The Zliten mosaic, discovered near the ruins of the Roman settlement at Leptis Magna in what is now Libya, and dated to the late first or early second century AD, shows a lion attacking a human. The statue of a lion standing on an animal was found in the ruins of the Roman garrison at Corbridge in northern England, dated to the first century, and is now the prize exhibit in the Corbridge museum. It is thought to depict the triumph of death over life. Four other lion statues have been discovered in the same area. Another statue of a lion, dated to the first century AD, was discovered in 1997 in a more northerly region of the Roman Empire at Cramond in Scotland, depicting a lioness devouring a human being. It is not difficult to see why Peter uses the image of a lion in describing the enemy. Clowney's comment is apropos:

> 'Our image of a roaring lion may come from visits to the zoo, or from the zoom lens of a television nature series. Some who received Peter's letter would have a stronger horror.

They had seen human blood dripping from the chops of lions in the gory spectacles of a Roman amphitheatre.'

However, not all in Rome itself suffered like that, as Clowney indicates by saying that 'some' did. Some in other parts of the empire also suffered as persecution spread from the centre. Lenski notes that, as the persecution intensified in Rome, 'The Roman authorities in the provinces would soon adopt the same attitude.' Peter, therefore, 'points them to others who are meeting the same ordeal', reminding his readers that knowledge of 'the same sufferings . . . experienced by your brotherhood in the world' would help them 'resist [the devil], steadfast in the faith' (1 Peter 5:9). The 'world', of course, is the world of the Roman Empire, which probably explains why statues of lions and other evidence of persecution dating from the first century are found in the outermost limits of the empire. Lenski translates 'resist' as 'stand against', and comments: 'This standing against the devil means refusal to deny Christ under threat of death.' Many Christians in Peter's day would have been able to testify to that.

> 'Defeat is not inevitable.' Christians are called to resist, 'expecting that the enemy will flee'.

One further observation seems appropriate. Grudem points out that the word 'resist' implies the possibility of victory. It reminds us of the words of James, 'Resist the devil and he will flee from you' (James 4:7). Grudem says that this command 'signifies that defeat is not inevitable'. Christians are called to resist, 'expecting that the enemy will flee'. Clowney adds, 'They can repulse the roaring lion: in the fires of trial their faith will not be destroyed, but purified like gold in the furnace.' Barclay argues that there is a law of Christian resistance. A Christian's faith must be 'like a solid wall against which the attacks of the devil exhaust themselves in vain'. It is true that in the early years of the Roman Empire many Christians resisted and perished. It is also true, as is now widely recognised, that many resisted and did not perish. Whoever they were, and how many there were, is to some extent immaterial. They all resisted, and in so doing remained 'steadfast in the faith'. And that is the bottom line.

One of Fanny Crosby's hymns helps to make Peter's challenging words about persecution, suffering, the enemy, resistance and steadfastness relevant to all End Time people today:

> *O Christian awake! 'Tis the Master's command,*
> *With helmet and shield,*
> *and a sword in thy hand,*
> *To meet the bold tempter; go, fearlessly go,*
> *Then stand like the brave,*
> *with thy face to the foe.*

For reflection and further study

From what we know about Peter, what life experiences shaped him to be able to write in his letter, 'But rejoice inasmuch as you participate in the sufferings of Christ, so that you may be overjoyed when his glory is revealed' (1 Peter 4:13, NIV)?

People who Hope

14

It was Alexander Pope, the renowned eighteenth-century English poet, who gave us the immortal line, 'Hope springs eternal within the human breast.' It is not merely a memorable line from a great poem, but is also the expression of a profound truth about the human psyche. To be human is to hope. Every day, millions of people around the world, consciously or subconsciously, live their lives in hope. They hope that it won't rain today, or that it will. They hope the train will be on time, or that they will not miss it. Some hope the stock market won't go down. Many hope that it will go up so that they can cash in. Others hope that the money they put on a certain team or horse will not turn out to have been wasted. The vast majority of human beings hope that the future will be better than the past, or even the present.

We all hope. We hope that our children will be safe at school, and on the way there and back. We hope that they will do well and go on to university. We hope that we and our families will keep healthy – and, perhaps, in the light of recent events, that some dreaded pandemic will not catch up with us. We hope for peace and prosperity; enough money to be able to live comfortably; and some perspicuity to be able to make the right decisions for ourselves and those who depend on us. And so we could go on. Hope, it seems, continues to spring eternal in every human breast.

Writing in *The Vocabulary of the Bible*, the French theologian J. P. Ramseyer comments on hope as a mark of our common humanity:

'In order to be able to live, it is essential to have a future. . . . Hope belongs to life. What does not yet exist largely conditions what is in the process of becoming. Thus, the things that we wait for, and our manner of waiting for them, partly make us what we are.'

Ramseyer is speaking particularly of Christian hope, and goes on to say, 'Hope is seizing in faith the promise of life and salvation.' He then reminds us, 'The believer's hope does not come from within himself,' as does so often the eternal hope of humanity which keeps so many going through the challenges and uncertainties of life.

> 'In order to be able to live, it is essential to have a future. . . . Hope belongs to life.'

In his article on the biblical meaning of hope, Ramseyer cites two texts from 1 Peter which are crucial to the entire New Testament teaching about hope: 1 Peter 1:3 and 4, and 1 Peter 1:21. One commentator says that hope is a 'key thought' in 1 Peter, so much so that the epistle 'may be called a letter of hope in the midst of suffering'. Peter uses the word 'hope' four times in the first epistle – five if we allow translations of verse 4 which use the word 'hope', such as J. B. Phillips, who begins verse 4 with the phrase, 'You can now hope . . .'. With one exception, all five appear in chapter one. It is as though Peter wants to reassure his readers of their hope at the beginning of the letter before he goes on to speak of the suffering and persecution which await them, and of their need for steadfastness in the face of such great trials. Commenting on verse 3 and the 'living hope' to which believers have been 'begotten' or reborn, Barclay makes a point that should not be overlooked: 'To the ancient world the Christian characteristic was hope.' To hope in the circumstances which Christians then endured was to bear witness to the watching world.

> To hope in the circumstances which Christians then endured was to bear witness to the watching world.

At the end of his second epistle Peter reminds them once more of the 'inheritance incorruptible and undefiled' (1 Peter 1:4) which awaits them in the world to come, saying that, according to God's promise, 'we . . . look for new heavens and a new earth' (2 Peter 3:13). In the next verse he says we are 'looking forward to these things'. The NIV uses the phrase 'looking forward' in verses 13 and 14, and the NLT uses 'looking forward' in verses 12 and 13. 'Looking forward' is an expression of hope, and there can be no doubt that in these verses Peter intentionally creates an atmosphere of hope for those who believe. Perhaps this is why Phillips translates verse 14 with this admonition: 'Because, my dear friends, you have a hope like this before you, I urge you to make certain that such a day would find you at peace with God and man.' So in this passage Peter ends his epistles as he began them, with a strong emphasis on hope, and with the reminder that the day is coming when 'everything will be destroyed', but that 'in keeping with his promise we are looking forward to a new heaven and a new earth' (verses 11 and 13, NIV).

> 'The hope of Christ's coming at the end of history is the logical and necessary outcome of our faith.'

The necessity of hope

In the first chapter of this book we referred to Steven Travis's book, *The Jesus Hope.* I first read it soon after publication, and I read it again in preparing this chapter, finding it still as relevant to Christians now as it was when first written. Travis began the book by saying, 'This is a book about hope, in days when hope is in short supply.' In a later book, *I Believe in the Second Coming of Christ,* Travis has a chapter entitled 'Christ Our Hope', in which he explains the nature and necessity of Christian hope in a way that demonstrates its centrality to the Christian message:

'The hope of Christ's coming at the end of history is the logical and necessary outcome of our faith that God has already acted for our salvation in the historical events of Jesus's life, death and resurrection. To remove the hope of a final consummation of what Jesus Christ began in history is to undermine the whole idea of God acting in history. God's plan of salvation worked out through history is (thus) left with a beginning and no end.'

To experience this hope and to participate in its proclamation are even more pressing necessities now than they were when Travis wrote these words.

> **The pen is still a powerful instrument in communicating the Gospel of hope.**

I recently came across a little book by Rudolf Schnackenburg, a German New Testament scholar, with the title: *Christ – Present and Coming.* In it he argues that today's increasing sense of hopelessness can be traced back to the early decades of the twentieth century, when pessimism about the future was already a widespread and growing problem. He cites the views of Bertrand Russell, a prominent and articulate atheist whose ideas shaped the thinking of many at the time, and whose influence and that of his followers is still clearly evident in much contemporary thought. Schnackenburg says:

'In his famous manifesto, "A Free Man's Worship", Bertrand Russell wrote: "Brief and powerless is man's life: on him and all his race the slow, sure doom falls pitiless and dark. Blind to good and evil, omnipotent matter rolls on its relentless way." '

Schnackenburg then comments, 'This is the consistent view of a materialistic view of the world.' As we have already noted, it is hardly necessary to say that Christian hope is even more essential now than it was in Russell's day or when Travis wrote about it. It is therefore encouraging, to say the least, to find that many voices are being raised today in defence of Christianity, and of the hope it provides and which must be proclaimed. The evidence comes, in part, from the titles of contemporary works which speak positively of hope as a defining characteristic of the Christian message, and of the responsibility of those who have it to share it: *The Jesus Hope; Reconciliation and Hope; Surprised by Hope; Grounds for Assurance and Hope; Hope When it Hurts;* and *The Hopeful Life,* to name a few. They have all been convincingly written after careful thought, and demonstrate that the pen is still a powerful instrument in communicating the Gospel of hope.

In what follows, we will examine three major reasons Peter proposes for the hope he has and wants his End Time readers to have. Together, they are the antidote for the world's present sickness – its pessimism; its nihilism; and the growing sense of purposelessness which pervades society, which drives so many to drink; to so-called 'pleasures' which at best are all transient; and, sadly, to suicide in increasing numbers, particularly among young people. We will find Peter's reasons as convincing and relevant as everything else he wrote and which we have examined in the foregoing chapters of this book.

The resurrection of Christ

The resurrection of Jesus is the first of the three reasons Peter gives as the basis of Christian hope. God 'according to His abundant mercy has begotten us again to a living hope *through the resurrection of Jesus Christ from the dead*' (1 Peter 1:3, emphasis supplied). In order for a person to be resurrected, he or she must first have died. The hope that Peter affirms, then, is based on two historical realities – the death of Jesus, and His subsequent resurrection. Peter speaks of both events in 1 Peter 1, linking them together as the basis for salvation and for hope (1 Peter 1:3, 9-11), resurrection clearly assuming His death. Michael Green wrote a book entitled *The Empty Cross of Jesus* to emphasise that Christ's death is just as important as His resurrection as a reason for hope, and that one cannot be understood without the other.

> **Christ's death is just as important as His resurrection as a reason for hope, and ... one cannot be understood without the other.**

That Peter was in tune here again with the rest of the New Testament is clear from the fact that every book in the New Testament declares or assumes that Christ rose from the dead. The earliest textual references to this monumental event outside the gospels are found in the book of Acts, where Peter's first sermons are recorded. His sermon on the Day of Pentecost, in which the crucifixion and resurrection were central, laid the foundation for others which followed (Acts

2:23, 24; 30-32). Peter had seen Jesus after the resurrection with his own eyes, as had more than five hundred other witnesses (1 Corinthians 15:5, 6). They all testified to what they had seen, and to what they believed was an historical event. A case at law in which more than five hundred witnesses bore testimony would be well-nigh impossible to overturn. This chapter was finished on Easter Monday, when the message of the resurrection was still a recent and vivid memory, and had brought to mind Charles Wesley's hymn, 'Christ the Lord Is Risen Today, Alleluia!'

> 'I know of no facts in the history of mankind which are proved by better or fuller evidence ... than that Christ died and rose again from the dead.'

Thomas Arnold, Professor of History at Oxford University and later the famous headmaster of Rugby School, where rugby football originated, wrote a three-volume history of ancient Rome. In it he declared, 'I know of no facts in the history of mankind which are proved by better or fuller evidence ... than that Christ died and rose again from the dead.' Peter was one of the many witnesses who, in the days of the Roman Empire, provided evidence for the resurrection he had witnessed, and it is no wonder that he found it so compelling.

In more recent times the resurrection of Christ as an historical fact has been challenged. Various alternative theories have been proposed by the uninformed or the uninclined. While this is not the place to recount them again, those who may be interested can find them in various publications and on many well-informed websites. The same is true of the many reasons why the resurrection of Christ is as much an historical fact as is His death, or the deaths of untold thousands in the Roman persecutions of the early church.

The reality of Christ's resurrection and its significance as a catalyst of hope still depends today, as it did in the first century, on the testimony of those who were there, who saw the risen Christ and testified to what they had seen. We leave the last word on this to Sir Edward Clarke, QC, an English barrister who frequently appeared in the High Court as defence counsel. He wrote,

'As a lawyer, I have made a prolonged study of the evidences for the first Easter. To me the evidence is conclusive, and over and over again in the High Court I have secured the verdict on evidence not nearly so compelling. I accept it unreservedly as the testimony of men to facts that they were able to substantiate.'

The second coming of Christ

Christ's second coming is the second major reason for hope in Peter's epistles. He says that at that day salvation will finally become a reality, and will no longer be a belief that often can be merely theoretical. Salvation is the central theme running through the entire passage which precedes Peter's exhortation to believers in 1 Peter 1:13: 'Set your hope on the grace to be brought to you when Jesus Christ is revealed' (NIV). It is mentioned three times in this passage, in each instance emphasising an aspect of salvation which Peter believes is important:

> 'Set your hope on the grace to be brought to you when Jesus Christ is revealed.'

1. In verses 5 and 7 salvation is 'ready to be revealed in the last time . . . at the revelation of Jesus Christ'. Salvation is clearly something that is not yet complete.
2. In verse 9 it is 'the end of your faith' ('end' used here in the sense of an objective or goal), and hence something to look forward to and hope for.
3. In verses 10 and 11 it was the concern of the Old Testament prophets who predicted 'the sufferings of Christ and the glories that would follow'. Full salvation, in Peter's day and in his thinking, is at hand; it was anticipated; and it had been predicted, as had the 'glories that would follow'.

Salvation is not only accomplished by Christ at Calvary, but is a process which culminates in the 'incorruptible inheritance' awaiting believers in 'heaven', after the 'revelation of Jesus Christ' at the last day. When Steven Travis wrote about 'Christ Our Hope' he had all this in mind, maybe more.

In Peter's view, however, there is more to it than that. His exhortation to hope must be read in context. Verse 13 begins with 'Therefore' – what follows is the consequence of all that has been said in the preceding passage concerning salvation (verses 3-12). It is clear enough. Belief in the salvation that will be completed at Christ's coming requires certain actions and attitudes on the part of those who are waiting. They are outlined in a series of imperatives in verses 13-15, ending with the seemingly impossible command, 'Be holy in all your conduct.' These challenging consequences of belief in Christ's coming are in part the answer to the question posed in 2 Peter 3:11, which has been the primary concern of this book: 'What manner of persons ought you to be' in view of the approaching day of the Lord? Peter's answer is that they are the kind of people who know that Christ is coming, even if they do not know precisely when, and who allow that knowledge to determine the way they live. They can then look forward with true hope to what is to come, and to the heavenly inheritance that awaits all who believe.

> 'What manner of persons ought you to be' in view of the approaching day of the Lord?

Berkouwer's comments are most helpful, particularly for those who might be apprehensive about their standing when Christ comes again:

> 'The end must never produce nervousness or anxiety, nor induce passivity or anxious preoccupation. . . . In his commentary on this passage, E. Selwyn describes this composure as "a cool head and a balanced mind, the opposite of all mania or individual excitement".'

He then states that the 'distinctiveness of the Christian expectation' of the future 'is characterised by joy, certainty, patience and sobriety'.

Travis emphasises that Christ's coming will bring about two things in particular: 'God will complete the plan He began in Christ,' and will 'bring history to a climax', resulting in the final establishment of God's kingdom. So, he says, 'We long for Christ's return' to bring all this about. He also reminds us that true Christian hope is not merely focused on the coming of an event, but on the coming of a Person, stressing 'the joyful fact' that this coming will be *'the coming of Christ'*:

'When we come to history's end we shall not face a distant, unknown figure. We shall encounter the same Person whose holiness, truth and utter love we already know in Christ. Written on the pages of history from beginning to end is love – personal, self-giving love – and it is that love which will meet us on the final day.'

So Peter reminds his readers, 'Your faith and hope are in God' (1 Peter 1:21), and 'if someone asks about your hope as a believer, always be ready to explain it' (1 Peter 3:15, NLT).

New heavens and a new earth
The end of history is, for those who have lived through Earth's tumultuous last days, the beginning of eternity. As creatures of time, it is difficult to conceive of an existence that is timeless. But that is what eternity is, even as God Himself is eternal. His new heavens and new earth are created after time, as we understand it, has ended. It seems that Peter may have had some conception of this when in the same chapter, 2 Peter 3, he advises his readers to remember that 'with the Lord one day is as a thousand years, and a thousand years as one day' (2 Peter 3:8).

Be that as it may, there is no uncertainty in Peter's mind of what is yet to come. Following the great day of the Lord and the dissolution of the very elements in fervent heat, Peter declares, 'But our hopes are set not on these but on the new Heaven and the new earth which he has promised us' (verse 13, Phillips). There is nothing here to make us think that this is symbolic language, as some have suggested. In support of his claim Peter quotes Isaiah 65:17 and 66:22; and, although John wrote the book of Revelation some thirty years or so later, Peter's conception of new heavens and a new earth, taken from Isaiah, was affirmed by John in Revelation 21 and 22. 'I saw a new heaven and a new earth, for the first heaven and the first earth had passed away' (Rev. 21:1). Our old friend Lenski, commenting on 2 Peter 3:13, writes:

> 'Written on the pages of history from beginning to end is love – personal, self-giving love – and it is that love which will meet us on the final day.'

> 'The old universe was spoiled by the fall. Sin permeated it with its effects. That includes all of nature, animate and inanimate, the heavenly bodies, and the heavens also. All shall become new. . . . The heavens and the earth shall be renovated, renewed, purified, made perfect.'

Whether or not Lenski had his cosmology quite right is to some extent beside the point. His understanding of the renovation and recreation of the earth is in harmony with that of Peter, Isaiah and John. Paradise Lost will become Paradise Regained. Significant as are Christ's resurrection and His second coming as reasons for hope, it is difficult to avoid the conclusion that the creation of new heavens and a new earth is the most compelling reason of all. It brings to mind the closing pages of Ellen White's *The Great Controversy*, where, in the light of biblical predictions of the world to come, she writes of the new earth and the existence of a new humanity:

> 'There, immortal minds will contemplate with never-failing delight the wonders of creative power. . . . Every faculty will be developed, and every capacity increased. . . . All the treasures of the universe will be open to the study of God's redeemed. Unfettered by mortality, they wing their tireless flight to worlds afar. . . .'

As End Time people living in the last of the last days, our minds should be fortified and our hearts cheered by the prospect of a new world soon to come. Sometimes we express our hope in that bright future: 'We have this hope,' we sing of Christ's coming. But perhaps the words of an older hymn are even more relevant. Attributed to Bernard of Cluny from the twelfth century and translated into English in the nineteenth century, and drawing on the imagery in the book of Revelation, they speak more specifically of the hope that arises from looking beyond the second coming to the glories of the earth made new:

People who Hope

Jerusalem the golden, with milk and honey blest,
Beneath thy contemplation sink heart and voice oppressed.
I know not, O I know not, what holy joys are there;
What radiancy of glory, what bliss beyond compare.

O sweet and blessed country, the home of God's elect!
O sweet and blessed country that eager hearts expect!
Jesus, in mercy bring us to that dear land of rest;
Who art with God the Father and the Spirit ever blest.

Nevil Shute's novel *On the Beach* and the subsequent movie were set in Victoria, Australia. A nuclear war had demolished much of the northern hemisphere, and a massive cloud of radioactive dust was drifting slowly but inexorably southwards towards the great southern land, bringing with it radiation, sickness and death. In the book and in the movie Mary and her husband Peter and many other Australians in Victoria live out those last doom-filled weeks before the deadly cloud arrives. Some comfort themselves with alcohol. Others pack as much pleasure-seeking into the remaining time as they can. Others go to church or attend open-air religious meetings for comfort. Peter plants a tree in the garden and buys a garden seat in the hope that somehow there will be a future. Mary, who is carrying their first child, cries out in despair, 'But there's got to be hope!'

'Jesus, in mercy bring us to that dear land of rest.'

Mary speaks for many thousands living today, more likely millions, who feel exactly the same. They see the news daily on TV, read the papers, see pictures of war, rebellion, death, disease, underfed orphans and displaced refugees; rising rates of depression and suicide, especially among young people; murder, violence and aggression in many countries around the world – and wonder if it is ever going to end. They cry out with Mary, 'But there's got to be hope!' The good news for every 'Mary' and 'Peter' on the planet, and for everyone else as well, is that there *is*. There *is* hope. And few present it with as much conviction or make clear its reality better than Peter. All who seek hope in this benighted world should read his epistles carefully, thoughtfully, and

'But there's got to be hope!'

frequently. They should ponder well the reasons Peter gives for hope as outlined in the pages above. The silver lining behind every dark cloud will soon become apparent, and life will truly be worth living. If hope no longer 'springs eternal' in every human breast today as once it did, it can, and does, arise and remain in the heart of every informed and believing Christian. And it must be proclaimed and shared.

For reflection and further study

It was C. S. Lewis who said in his book *Mere Christianity*, 'It is since Christians have largely ceased to think of the other world that they have become so ineffective in this. Aim at Heaven and you'll get the earth "thrown in": aim at earth and you'll get neither.' Read through 2 Peter 3, keeping in mind what Lewis says. How does living a hope-filled life give purpose for living in the here and now?

People who Witness 15

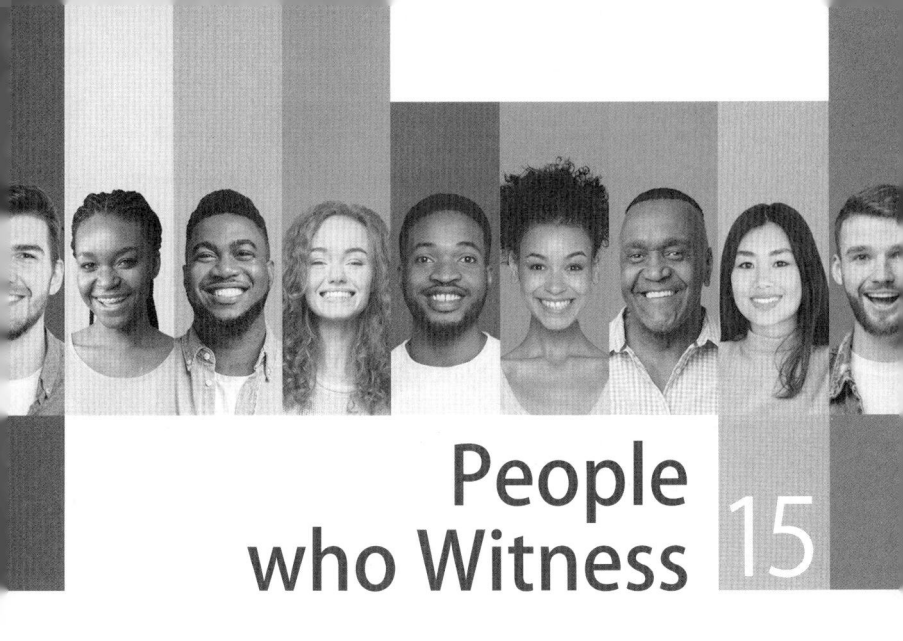

There were three major events in Peter's life which would have left an indelible impression on him, making him who he was and informing what he preached and wrote. The first event, as recorded in Mark 1:16 and 17, is that he was one of four fishermen Jesus called from their nets by the Sea of Galilee with the promise that He would make them 'fishers of men'. The second experience occurred three years later, after the resurrection and again by the Sea of Galilee, when Jesus gave Peter a specific mission: 'Feed My sheep.' Peter was not only to be a fisher of men: he was also to be a shepherd. He would never forget either of these charges, for they were the foundation on which he built the rest of his life. The third experience would have come as a final confirmation of the mission to which he had been divinely called. He and the other disciples heard Christ's last words before He returned to heaven: 'Go therefore and make disciples of all the nations' (Matthew 28:19). Luke's account reads, 'You shall receive power when the Holy Spirit has come upon you; and you shall be witnesses to Me in Jerusalem, and in all Judea and Samaria, and to the end of the earth' (Acts 1:8). It is self-evident that the 'Great Commission', as it has come to be known, is as relevant to End Time people today as it was to Peter and the other

> 'Go therefore and make disciples of all the nations.'

disciples. It is still a binding obligation on all believers – the Church's marching orders, in fact. In the power of the Spirit the early church, under Peter's leadership, grew at a phenomenal rate, rapidly spreading out from Jerusalem until it was known across the ancient world.

There is, however, a challenge here. Michael Green, in the preface to Max Warren's book, *I Believe in the Great Commission*, begins by saying, 'Contemporary Christianity has, for the most part, lost its nerve.' He goes on to say that, in the context of relativism, agnosticism, apathy and syncretism,

> 'To maintain that Christianity is true, that Jesus really is the way to God, and that obedience to Him inevitably carries with it the imperative to mission, is thoroughly unpopular.'

> **It is the necessity of a compassionate society, and for the Church to be involved in the creation of that society.**

That was written in 1976, but I make no apology for citing it here, for it is still as relevant now as it was then. I have found it necessary in the process of writing this book to defend my use of sources now largely regarded as out of date. As I have said previously, new does not necessarily mean better. Max Warren's book is a compelling illustration of the fact that now, as in his day, the present generation have lost sight of the works of older writers, if they ever even knew them, and we and the Church as a whole are the poorer for it. To believe in the Great Commission is just as necessary now as it was Peter's day and in Max Warren's day, and will remain so until the last sermon has been preached, the last book written and the last lost sheep brought home.

The very first necessity, in Warren's view, for the recovery of nerve and successful witnessing to contemporary society is found in the section of the book, 'What Spelling It Out Today Means'. It is the necessity of a compassionate society, and for the Church to be involved in the creation of that society. To churches who have thought that words, written or spoken, are the first essential for successful witnessing, this may come as something of a surprise, even a rebuke. Perhaps ADRA, Asian Aid, the Salvation Army and other like-minded entities are more essential than evangelistic programmes or sermons.

There is much more in Warren's *I Believe in the Great Commission* that is relevant. But enough said. We must now return to Peter and what he says about witnessing to a secular or hostile world.

Fulfilling God's purposes

Peter's first reference to witnessing reminds his readers, in Old Testament terms and imagery, that God's redemptive purposes for the world were to be worked out through His people. Peter's first readers and those who were to come after them were a chosen people, just as Israel had been: the appointed means through which the good news of God's grace and love would be made known to the surrounding culture. After Israel's dismal failure, it was the divine plan that the world would be reached through the Church. So Peter writes to those first Christian believers, God's new Israel:

> 'You are a chosen generation, a royal priesthood, a holy nation, His own special people, *that you may proclaim the praises of Him who called you out of darkness into His marvelous light*' (1 Peter 2:9, emphasis supplied).

> Peter chose his words well when he reminded the early Christians of their responsibility to make known the excellencies of God.

The word 'that' indicates a consequence and a reason. Peter's readers – including us – were specifically chosen to proclaim what God had done for them.

There are two rare Greek words which, under inspiration, Peter uses here. The word translated 'proclaim' comes from a Greek word which is only used once in the New Testament, by Peter in this text. It literally means 'to tell forth', 'to proclaim boldly': 'to tell it as it is', as we might say today. Most modern English versions translate it as 'proclaim', which carries those connotations. The word for 'praises' in the original means 'virtues', 'excellence' or 'excellencies'. Souter notes that it was 'a word of wide significance in non-Christian ethics' of the time. It seems that Peter chose his words well when he reminded the early Christians of their responsibility to make known the excellencies of God to the surrounding non-Christian cultures of the day.

Verse 12 throws further light on God's intentions and His

people's witnessing responsibilities. In fact, verse 9 can only properly be understood in the light of verses 11 and 12. Peter implores those who read or heard his letter:

'Beloved, I beg you as sojourners and pilgrims, abstain from fleshly lusts which war against the soul, *having your conduct honorable among the Gentiles . . .*' (emphasis supplied).

'Gentiles' is used here as an inclusive term for all who are not Christians: that is, for both literal Jews and literal Gentiles. Grudem points out that Peter's counsel here 'refers to a day-to-day pattern of life', and Clowney explains that Peter is 'concerned about their lifestyle as resident aliens, and about their witness to those among whom they live', adding that 'God's people must be aliens in a world of rebels against God'. J. B. Phillips translates verse 12 in his own refreshing way:

'Your conduct among the surrounding peoples in your different countries should always be good and right, so that although they may in the usual way slander you as evil-doers yet when disasters come, they may glorify God when they see how well you conduct yourselves.'

Peter does not say that the pagans who observe the way Christians behave *will* glorify God, but that they *may* do. Even if only a few do so, then the outcome will surely be pleasing to God and to the Church. The point not to be overlooked is that it is lifestyle, conduct, which Peter advocates as the most effective way to witness. We shall see this emphasis repeated as we read what Peter wrote later in the epistle. Barclay says: 'The striking fact of history is that by their lives the Christians actually did defeat the slanders of the heathen.' End Time people would do well to remember this counsel from Peter and the consequent lessons from history. It would save a lot of wasted energy, time and money if we all practised what Peter says is God's chosen way to witness, and it might be said that the outcome would be much better.

The effect of a Christian lifestyle

Verse 13 in the NKJV begins with 'Therefore....' What follow in the rest of chapter two and on into chapter three are consequences of the injunction in verse 12 to live honourably before the Gentiles. Peter's point is that submissiveness is an important characteristic of such a lifestyle. We need to follow him closely here. Clowney explains that in these verses 'Peter describes Christian living in terms of submission: submission to one another as Christians, and especially to unbelievers.' Peter specifies the submission of citizens to governments and the submission of servants to their masters, both indications of a lifestyle that is pleasing to God, which exemplifies Christ's submissiveness to the will of God, and which speaks silently to the unconverted Gentiles (1 Peter 2:13-25). We should note that submissiveness is not the same as subjection. It is rather the result of a willing mind to do God's will: in this case, to choose a Christian lifestyle, one that is radically different from that of the surrounding non-Christian culture.

Peter then begins chapter three by considering another practical situation, the challenge of a marriage between a believer and an unbeliever.

> 'Wives, likewise, be submissive to your own husbands, that even if some do not obey the word, they, without a word, may be won by the conduct of their wives' (1 Peter 3:1).

> **Submissiveness to the will of God ... speaks silently to the unconverted Gentiles (1 Peter 2:13-25). We should note that submissiveness is not the same as subjection. It is rather the result of a willing mind to do God's will.**

That Peter should raise this matter – which today would be regarded as contentious, if not downright sexist – is probably an indication that such situations were not uncommon in the first-century church. Furthermore, he would probably have agreed that the same applied to husbands with unbelieving wives.

In his *Introduction and Commentary on First Peter*, Grudem examines this passage at some length, concluding:

> 'Unbelieving husbands can be won without a word – that is, not by continually preaching or talking about the Gospel,

but rather simply *by the behaviour of their wives,* their Christian pattern of life.... Though Peter does not exactly say that Christians should never talk about the gospel message to their unbelieving husbands or friends, he does indicate that the means God will use to win such persons will generally not be words, but behaviour.'

A classic example is the experience of John Bunyan, whom we first met in chapter 8. He describes in graphic terms his early life as the filthy-mouthed ringleader of the local yobs: 'I had but few equals, both for cursing, lying, and blaspheming the holy name of God.' But at the age of twenty-one he married a girl who was so poor that she could only bring to the marriage as dowry two books. They were two of the best-known spiritual guides of the time. Bunyan was teaching himself to read and write, and as he read these books a great change took place in his life. Realising from what he read and from the example of his wife's life that he was far from God, he turned over a new leaf and became, instead of a constantly inebriated lout, one of the most well-known Christian apologists of all time, writing more than sixty books and preaching whenever and wherever the opportunity arose. It is said that his most well-known book, *Pilgrim's Progress,* sold over 100,000 copies in his lifetime, has never been out of print since, and has been translated into more than 200 languages. None of this would have happened, and the world would have been immeasurably poorer, but for his marriage in 1648 to a destitute but devoted Christian wife.

The witness of words

The emphasis Peter gives to lifestyle witnessing in the first three chapters of his first epistle should not be taken to mean that he has no time for verbal witnessing. He makes that clear when he says, 'Always be prepared to give an answer to everyone who asks you to give the reason for the hope that you have' (1 Peter 3:15, NIV). An answer can only be given in writing or by word of mouth.

The Greek word for 'answer' is *apologia* – in English, 'apology' – in the sense of 'explanation' or 'defence'. In either case, words are required. The NLT translation of the text reads, 'If someone asks about your hope as a believer, always be ready to explain it.' Barclay says that it was inevitable, in a hostile and suspicious world, that Christians would be called upon to defend the faith. It might well be asked, 'Why should anyone in the pagan or Gentile world of the first century ask a Christian about his or her belief?' There were several possible reasons why this could happen, and several questions that could be asked:

> **'Always be prepared to give an answer.'**

- Why did they believe things that were 'foolishness to the Greeks' and a 'stumbling block to the Jews' (see 1 Corinthians 1:23-25)?
- Would they be able to defend the faith before a Roman court?
- Why were they willing to be thrown to lions in the Colosseum or a similar arena in the Roman Empire?
- What exactly did they hope for?
- And why did they hope at all, in a world or in a life that had no future?

It was more likely that Christians would be put on the spot than be given notice of any of these questions. That is why they were to be 'always ready' to give an immediate and appropriate answer. Also, as Clowney rightly points out, 'Unbelievers may become enquirers, asking with more than curiosity about the distinctive Christian hope.' Whatever the motive driving the questions, Peter's counsel stands: 'Always be prepared to give an answer.' It is more easily said than done, as many have discovered from personal experience.

It should also be remembered that when Peter enjoins the use of words as well as lifestyle in witnessing, he is again speaking in harmony with the whole biblical revelation. The words 'proclaim', 'proclamation' and 'declare' appear repeatedly throughout the Old Testament, as do other references to words, speech and language, as for example in Psalm 19:1-3, NIV 1984:

'The heavens declare the glory of God;
the skies proclaim the work of his hands.
Day after day they pour forth speech;
night after night they display knowledge.
There is no speech or language
where their voice is not heard.
Their voice goes out into all the earth,
their words to the ends of the world.'

> 'The Christian must go through the mental and spiritual toil of thinking out his faith, so that he can tell what he believes and why.'

Beyond the cosmological implications of this powerful passage, its metaphorical use of the necessity of words in communication is beyond compare.

Barclay further states that, in responding to questions about their faith, Christians must give reasonable and intelligent answers. He then makes the application, uncomfortable as it may be, and as relevant now as it was in the first century:

'To do so, we must know what we believe; we must have thought it out; we must be able to state it intelligently and intelligibly. Our faith must be a first-hand discovery and not a second-hand story. It is one of the tragedies of the modern situation that there are so many church members who, if they were asked what they believe, could not tell, and who, if they were asked why they believe it, would be equally helpless. The Christian must go through the mental and spiritual toil of thinking out his faith, so that he can tell what he believes and why.'

The success of the early church may be put down to the fact that its members knew all this, and that most of them put it into practice.

We must return now to the Great Commission and Christ's directive to the disciples just before He returned to heaven after His resurrection. The commission included 'teaching' people from all nations. The Greek word is *didasko* (from which we get the word 'didactic'), meaning 'instruction'. Teaching cannot take place without using words, and it was Christ's command to be carried out, as Phillips says (Matthew 28:20), 'to the end of the world' – or, in terms that might be better understood today, 'until the end of time'. In Max Warren's book, *I Believe in the Great Commission*, cited earlier in this chapter, he says: 'Obeying the Great Commission today and tomorrow will be no easier than in the past.' Yet it must be done, as Peter knew well enough, since he was present when Jesus gave the disciples their orders, which were to extend until time was no longer. Warren says that the Great Commission and the entire New Testament from Matthew to Revelation 'were not written to be explained away'. Warren could not have known when he wrote these words that this was just what would happen. It has been claimed that today 51% of evangelical Christians 'don't understand or have forgotten what the Great Commission is'. Conversely, this means that many have remembered and do understand. The task incumbent on every Christian and on the entire Church is the same as it has always been. It is to declare 'the truth, the whole truth, and nothing but the truth'. As the words of the Great Commission indicate, it must be communicated verbally to all people in their own language and in words they can understand.

> It must be communicated verbally to all people in their own language and in words they can understand.

In a manner of speaking

It is a well-understood axiom of successful communication that it is not only what is said that matters, but also how it is said. In the text we have been considering, 1 Peter 3:15, it is clear that Peter recognised the importance of this principle. He says, 'Always be prepared to give an answer to everyone who asks you to give the reason for the hope that you have. *But do this with gentleness and respect . . .*' (NIV). The footnote in the NIV says, 'Our apologetic (answer) is always to be given with love, never in degrading terms.' The effectiveness of the answer we give to anyone who wants to know what we believe will be determined in part by

> We are not salesmen, but witnesses. Those who follow Peter's counsel do not come across as 'pushy' or self-assertive.

how we speak. We are not salesmen, but witnesses. Those who follow Peter's counsel do not come across as 'pushy' or self-assertive, or speak in an aggressive manner, as is so easily the case with people who are convinced that they are right; and they are at the same time always mindful of the role of the Holy Spirit in bringing people to faith.

Barclay makes these perceptive comments, suggesting that he is speaking from experience:

'There are many people who state their beliefs with a kind of arrogant belligerence. Their attitude is that anyone who does not agree with them is either a fool or a knave, and they seek to ram their beliefs down other people's throats. The case for Christianity must be presented with winsomeness and love, and with that wise tolerance which realises that it is not given to any man to possess the whole truth.'

> **'The case for Christianity must be presented with winsomeness and love.'**

It is unnecessary to say more. All that remains now is for those who read these words to put them and everything else Peter says about witnessing into practice. We might be pleasantly surprised by the result. We might also like to use the lovely words of a hymn we do not often sing as a prayer for ourselves and our fellow believers, that we may all witness effectively:

Lord of all nations, grant me grace
to love all people, every race,
And in each person may I see
my kindred loved, redeemed by Thee.

Break down the wall that would divide
Thy children, Lord, on every side.
My neighbour's good let me pursue;
let Christian love bind, warm and true.

Forgive me, Lord, where I have erred
by loveless act or thoughtless word.
Make me to see the wrong I do
will crucify my Lord anew.

*Give me the courage, Lord, to speak
whenever the strong oppress the weak.
Should I myself the victim be,
help me forgive, rememb'ring Thee.*

*With Thine own love may I be filled,
and by Thy Holy Spirit willed,
That all I touch, where'er I be,
may be divinely touched by Thee.*

For reflection and further study

'Because actions speak louder than words, I would rather witness through my actions than tell someone about who Jesus is.' While this is understandable in these sceptical times, why is it also important, as Peter instructs, to 'always be prepared to give an answer to everyone who asks you to give the reason for the hope that you have' (1 Peter 3:15, NIV)?

16 The End Time

Most of this book was written in 2020, the year that will be remembered for the COVID-19 pandemic which has swept the world, causing social and economic upheaval on a scale unprecedented in modern times. At the time of writing, July 2021, it is still raging around the world with no end yet in sight, having already claimed nearly four million lives, with 183,000,000 active cases in 219 countries and territories, and new and more virulent variants in many parts of the world, where in some places the demands for hospital care can hardly be met. Many thinking people have seen it as a fulfilment of Christ's description of the End Time as one of 'distress' among nations, with 'perplexity' and 'men's hearts failing them from fear and the expectation of those things which are coming on the earth' (Luke 21:25, 26). Recent messages from friends and relatives have told of loved ones lost and of uncertainty and anxiety about the future. Reports of an increase in Bibles being sold and people turning to prayer for comfort have been around for months now. With all this in mind, we must now consider what Peter says about the End Time and the conditions which will then prevail, many of which already prevailed as he wrote.

> Many thinking people have seen it as a fulfilment of Christ's description of the End Time.

It was noted at the beginning of this book that, with the exception of one chapter (2 Peter 3), End Time events were not on Peter's agenda. That one exception is of immense significance for End Time people today. Peter begins this final chapter of his epistles with a reminder: 'I want you to recall the words spoken in the past by the holy prophets and the command given by our Lord and Saviour through your apostles' (2 Peter 3:2, NIV). Michael Green, whom we have quoted several times in the previous chapters of this book, says of this text:

> 'The meaning is clear enough, and stresses the link between the prophets who foreshadowed Christian truth, Christ who exemplified it, and the apostles who gave an authoritative interpretation of it.'

Peter then continues in the next verse: 'Above all, you must understand that in the last days scoffers will come, scoffing and following their own evil desires' (verse 3, NIV). It may well be that Peter has in mind the false prophets he scathingly denounces in chapter two, who 'secretly bring in destructive heresies' and 'walk according to the flesh in the lust of uncleanness and despise authority . . . having eyes full of adultery and that cannot cease from sin' (2 Peter 2:2, 10, 14). They 'bring on themselves swift destruction . . . and will utterly perish in their own corruption' (2 Peter 2:1, 12). Peter clearly has little time or patience for these people. We will come to the substance of their scoffing shortly, but first of all we must, as Peter exhorts, 'understand' what kind of people they are who scoff, and whose mocking Peter says is a sign of the End Time. They have at least two related problems – they are immoral, and they are cynical. Lenski calls them 'libertinists', who live lives of 'moral laxity'. Michael Green points out that they mock and at the same time live self-indulgent lives, and explains:

> 'Cynicism and self-indulgence regularly go together. These men do not mock merely because the second coming has been delayed; they laugh at the very idea. . . . Anthropocentric hedonism always mocks at the idea of

ultimate standards and a final division between the saved and the lost. For men who live in the world of the relative, the claim that the relative will be ended by the absolute is nothing short of ludicrous.'

It is not difficult to see the parallel between Peter's world and the world we live in today. In 1996, Robert Bork wrote a book with the intriguing title, *Slouching Towards Gomorrah*. Bork was a constitutional lawyer who taught law at Yale University Law School and was Solicitor General of the United States and a Court of Appeals judge. Commenting on the moral decline of the West as reflected in American culture, Bork said that already 'the distinctive features of Western civilisation are in peril in ways not previously seen', commenting:

'Large chunks of the moral life of the United States, major features of its culture, have disappeared altogether, and more are in the process of extinction. They are being replaced by new modes of conduct, ways of thought, and standards of morality that are unwelcome to many of us. The rap beat blasts out of the car waiting beside you at a red light; blatant sexuality, often of a perverse nature, assaults the reader in magazine advertisements; carnage is promised in motion picture advertisements. Popular entertainment sells sex, pornography, violence, vulgarity, attacks on traditional forms of authority, and outright perversion more copiously and more insistently than ever before in our history.'

> 'The distinctive features of Western civilisation are in peril in ways not previously seen.'

He concluded, 'We must, then, take seriously the possibility that perhaps nothing will be done to reverse the direction of our culture, that the degeneracy we see about us will only become worse.' Twenty-five years on, he would have been in no doubt at all.

The attack on Christ's second coming

The main focus of the scoffers' mockery is the second coming of Christ. The reason they give is that nothing has changed. The world goes on as it has done for millennia: 'All things continue as they were from the beginning' (2 Peter 3:4). Their argument is, in today's language, that the world continues in a stable universe, an unchanging system, in which divine intervention of any kind does not take place. Miracles and events like the second coming just do not happen. So they scoff at the idea. Barclay rightly says that there were, in fact, two arguments which the scoffers brought against the belief that Christ would come again:

> 'Their first argument was that the promise had been so long delayed that it was safe to take it that it would never be fulfilled. Their second assertion was that their fathers had died and the world was going on precisely as it always did . . . this was characteristically a stable universe, and convulsive upheavals like the second coming did not happen in such a universe.'

The similarity between first-century scoffers and those who appeared like a swarm of disturbed bees in the middle of the twentieth century is again remarkable. In defence of the traditional second-advent hope, A. L. Moore points out in his carefully researched book, *The Parousia in the New Testament*, that many modern New Testament scholars in America and Europe, including England, contributed at that time to the demise of the original New Testament hope, including C. H. Dodd, J. A. T. Robinson, T. F. Glasson, J. Jeremias and R. Bultmann, to name a few. Bultmann proposed that the entire New Testament should be 'demythologised', while others advanced the idea of a 'realised eschatology', which holds that the second coming had already taken place in the Person of Christ and that there was no need for Him to come again. The arguments of these respected biblical scholars were influential at the time, and have been perpetuated by others who followed them. Those who have read this book through will recall that I met one of their prominent converts at an interdenominational conference in the 1970s and was astonished at his disbelief in the second coming. He had moved on in his thinking, and quite likely would have had a very different interpretation of 2 Peter 3.

Deliberate forgetfulness and willing ignorance
After introducing the scoffers who ridicule the idea of the second coming, Peter continues in verse 5 with an accusation suggesting dishonesty: 'But they deliberately forget that long ago by God's word the heavens came into being and the earth was formed out of water and by water' (NIV). Deliberate forgetfulness is one of two related mindsets that contribute to the dishonest attitude of the scoffers. These people knew the facts about Creation and the Flood and chose not to remember them. This was not an oversight. It is hard to fathom how anyone can really forget things of such significance that they once knew. Perhaps it might be better to say that they put these facts at the back of their minds and pretended that they had never known them. A similar situation prevails today. The Old Testament teachings of Creation and the Flood were among the first casualties of the demythologisation of the Bible, and are – despite credible evidence to the contrary – now widely regarded as stories intended to teach or illustrate a truth without being literally true. Deliberate forgetfulness is a culpable way of thinking: 'reserved for fire until the day of judgment and perdition of ungodly men' (verse 7).

The second mindset, which is equally culpable, is that of willing ignorance, choosing not to examine the evidence which is readily available. It is a classic illustration of the old adage, 'The capacity to believe what one wants to believe is infinite.' One of the most audacious examples of willing ignorance is that of Richard Lewontin's attitude to reality in the face of available facts. Lewontin was a high-profile evolutionary biologist and geneticist at Harvard University. He admitted a prior commitment to atheism and a willingness to accept the priority of these presuppositions in the most unambiguous language:

'We take the side of science in spite of the patent absurdity of some of its constructs, in spite of its failure to fulfil many of its extravagant promises of health and life, in spite of the tolerance of the scientific community for unsubstantiated just-so stories, *because we have a prior commitment to materialism*. It is not that the methods and institutions of science somehow compel us to accept a material explanation of the phenomenal world, but, on the contrary, we are forced by our *a priori adherence to material causes* to create an apparatus of investigation and a set of concepts that produce material explanations, no matter how mystifying to the uninitiated. Moreover, *that materialism is absolute, for we cannot allow a Divine Foot in the door*' (emphases supplied).

The evidence for the weaknesses of evolutionary theory, the gaping holes in many of its arguments, and the scientific evidence of the impossibility of many of its claims are readily available from many sources for those who really want to know the truth. Lewontin was one of the majority who do not want to know. The relevance of Peter's comments on the scoffers of his day to our own time is quite remarkable.

The Creation and Flood accounts

Peter links Creation and the Flood together in 2 Peter 3:3-6, treating them as historical events, as did Jesus (on more than one occasion, it should not be forgotten). Peter was not aware of the findings of modern science, and could not know that in the last days of the End Time Creation and the Flood would be linked together not only in the Genesis text, but also by tangible evidence that would stand up to critical investigation. It would take volumes to present all the evidence available from archaeology, palaeontology and geology in support of the Genesis Flood, some of which has been known for centuries, as can be seen from the title of a remarkable cuneiform document discovered in the ruins of ancient Nineveh, written by Ashurbanipal, king of Assyria in the seventh century BC: *I Studied Inscriptions from Before the*

Flood. His personal library contained editions of earlier Creation and Flood accounts from various regions of the ancient world.

It has been suggested that such early Creation and Flood accounts, as in Ashurbanipal's record, might be 'myths', and therefore not evidence that these events really occurred, as they are said to have done in Ashurbanipal's account and in the scholarly book edited by Richard Hess and David Tsumura, which uses Ashurbanipal's claim as its title. On the surface it is a persuasive argument. However, it must be noted that several of the contributors to this book speak of 'the Great Flood' which occurred as a punishment for the rebellion of all humanity: 'the guilt of man', to quote one contributor. Another contributor considers Creation and the Flood together as 'a continuous narrative of the first era of human history', and yet another says, 'For the ancient Mesopotamians the Flood was a once-and-for-all cosmic event.' Peter certainly regarded it as such, and used it as an historical illustration of the final destruction of mankind and the earth (2 Peter 3:3-7). Morris and Whitcomb, in *The Genesis Flood*, make the following comment:

> 'The third chapter of Second Peter provides powerful New Testament support for the geographical universality of the Flood. Anything less than a catastrophe of such proportions would upset the entire force of Peter's argument and would give much encouragement to those he so solemnly warned.'

The following is a partial list of compelling geographical and geophysical evidence of a worldwide flood found to this day in many continents:
- The bone fissures of Europe and North America
- The frozen mammoths of Siberia and Alaska
- Inland lakes and old shore lines at high altitudes
- Fossil evidence of a universal climate in the past
- Evidence of previous extensive underwater activity on many continents
- Abundant marine sediments and fossils on land

- Abnormally abundant fossil distribution
- The remarkable and detailed preservation of fossils, including some with soft tissue
- Large fossil herds of dinosaurs, as large as ten thousand, killed and buried rapidly by some catastrophic event

Documentation of many of the above, and much else besides, can be found in publications such as A. M. Rehwinkel, *The Flood*; J. C. Whitcomb and H. M. Morris, *The Genesis Flood*; D. C. Read, *Dinosaurs: An Adventist View*; and Ariel A. Roth, 'The Genesis Flood and the Geological Record', in: Bryan W. Ball, ed., *In the Beginning: Science and Scripture Confirm Creation*. It is justifiable to think that Peter, had he known of the vast amount of evidence that would come to light in the future affirming what he himself had written, would have been greatly encouraged and grateful that End Time people would read his epistles with confidence and renewed faith.

The destruction of the earth
Having reminded his readers that the Creation and the Flood were brought about 'by the word of God', Peter now turns his attention to the future: 'By the same word the present heavens and earth are reserved for fire, being kept for the day of judgment and destruction of the ungodly' (2 Peter 3:7, NIV). Three times between verses 7 and 12 Peter predicts that the earth will again be destroyed as it was in Noah's day, this time by fire. Lenski correctly says, 'The flood is a type of the last judgement.' This, as we have seen, is good reason to believe that the Flood was universal, and not a local inundation, as many have come to think. The fires of the last day will destroy 'both the earth and the works that are in it', and even 'the elements will melt with fervent heat' (verses 10, 12). This final, refining conflagration will occur at 'the day of the Lord', which will 'come as a thief in the night'. There is no room here for doubt or misunderstanding.

The destruction of the earth is not an easy concept for the modern mind to accept, any more than is a universal flood. Yet, as in the case with the Genesis Flood, there is persuasive evidence that supports its credibility. Michael Green says that the imagery of Peter's description of the destruction of the world in a fiery conflagration 'is as relevant and powerful today as it was then'. He then goes on to explain what he means:

> 'Mankind cannot presume on the stability of the world. We cannot take for granted that our environment will continue to make possible human life. The forces of nature retain their primeval destructive power; nuclear weaponry makes the literal fulfilment of Peter's apocalyptic picture of cosmic conflagration not only possible, but the daily background of our lives.'

The nuclear aspirations of unpredictable rogue states like North Korea and Iran make the outlook of even greater concern. The picture is further complicated by the arrival of a deadly worldwide pandemic caused by a mutating virus that is predicted to get worse before it gets better, vaccines notwithstanding. Realistically, the destruction of the earth and everything upon it is a distinct possibility, and not the uninformed ravings of an unbalanced visionary. Peter brings some hope with his assertion that the Day of the Lord will come, at which time salvation becomes a final reality and the faithful receive their just reward. In the short term, however, for many the future looks 'nasty, brutish and short', to quote the seventeenth-century philosopher Thomas Hobbes.

There is a passage in the book of Revelation which for today's End Time people throws further light on the final destruction of the earth. It refers to the time when, in words immortalised in Handel's Hallelujah Chorus, 'The kingdoms of this world have become the kingdom of our Lord and of His Christ.' John wrote:

> 'The nations were angry, and Your wrath has come, and the time of the dead, that they should be judged, and that You

should reward Your servants the prophets and the saints, and those who fear Your name, small and great, *and should destroy those who destroy the earth*' (Rev. 11:18, emphasis supplied).

It is clearly the same time which Peter describes in 2 Peter 3, but with the additional clarification that God destroys 'those who destroy the earth'. It is a phrase which only in recent times has become fully understood. The threat of nuclear war has been hanging over the human race for more than half a century, and shows no sign of abating yet. But there is more here than the possibility of nuclear annihilation. The Greek verb translated 'destroy' in this text has many meanings: to corrupt, to damage, to mar and to spoil. It means that God will intervene when men are in the process of corrupting or spoiling the earth in the sense of damaging it beyond repair. The NLT translation of the phrase in Revelation 11:18 is, 'It is time to destroy all who have caused destruction on the earth,' and Phillips suggests a subtle but important difference when he describes them as 'those who destroy the earth'.

God will intervene.

There is yet more. We have already been reminded of the widespread moral corruption of our time in Robert Bork's comments quoted earlier in this chapter. There are others, too numerous to mention, who have come to similar conclusions. Bork's book was introduced by W. B. Yeats's poem, *The Second Coming*, in which, prior to that great event:

> *Things fall apart; the centre cannot hold;*
> *Mere anarchy is loosed upon the world,*
> *The blood-dimmed tide is loosed,*
> *and everywhere*
> *The ceremony of innocence is drowned;*
> *The best lack all conviction, while the worst*
> *Are full of passionate intensity.*

Bork said that this was one of the most-quoted poems of the time, a fact to which many others, including prominent people of the day, testified. Bork himself said of Yeats's poem, which

> **There is abundant and increasing evidence that it is taking place.**

had been written in 1919: 'He can hardly have had any conception of just how thoroughly things would fall apart as the centre failed to hold in the last third of this century. He can hardly have foreseen that passionate intensity, uncoupled from morality, would shred the fabric of Western culture.'

That moral corruption is a major mark of the End Time cannot be disputed.

The destruction of the environment has also been a growing worldwide concern in recent years. There is abundant and increasing evidence that it is taking place on the land, in the oceans and in the atmosphere. The end of time is no longer merely a theological possibility. It has become an environmental probability. Jess Moody, the Baptist minister who founded the interdenominational Palm Beach Atlantic University in 1968 and authored several books, and who openly opposed Donald Trump in a convention speech in 2018, is credited with saying, 'Someone called our time an elephant hanging from a cliff with its tail tied to a daisy.'

Few have done more to warn the world of the damage caused by environmental pollution and its irreversible effects on biodiversity than David Attenborough, whose traditional emphasis on evolution has been balanced somewhat by his concern for the planet's future rather than its past. His recent (2018) DVD, *Seven Worlds, One Planet,* contains enough evidence to convince anyone with an open mind of the undeniable fact that time is rapidly running out if our planet is to be saved. Too much destruction has already taken place, and too many species which rely on each other for survival have already been destroyed. The rate of deforestation and the elimination of species must be contained, he argues, if Planet Earth is to survive.

A few examples must suffice. Attenborough pointed out in 2018 that a third of the forests in Southern Asia had been lost in the previous ten years due to clearing for cultivation. The population of whale sharks in the seas around Indonesia has declined so rapidly in recent years that they are now a protected species. In 1956 there were approximately 175,000 orangutans in the forests of Borneo. Since 1995 the population has almost halved due to deforestation which has destroyed the homes of many, with only small patches of forest now remaining. Ninety-five per cent of Columbia's forests have disappeared to make room for agriculture and food production, leaving thousands of Tamarind monkeys cut off from the rest of their species. There used to be 50,000 species of insects in Columbian forests, but their number has fallen dramatically in the past couple of decades. Africa's dwindling White Rhinoceros population is now on the verge of extinction. In recent years, Attenborough claims, forest areas the size of a football field have disappeared every minute. It is a staggering estimation. Similar conditions are found on every continent.

Attenborough's most recent documentary for the BBC, *Extinction: The Facts*, was released in September 2020. It tells us that, worldwide, more than a million species are now at risk of extinction, and that the crisis of decreasing biodiversity has consequences for us all, including the risk of future pandemic diseases. It tells us that the animal and plant extinction rate is now approximately a hundred times faster than at any previous time in history. The *Observer* newspaper in the UK gave the film a 5-star rating, calling it 'essential television'.

There is more that Peter could not have known about, but which possibly he would have mentioned if he had. Climate change and global warming are two undeniable developments in this End Time in which we now live. For those with open minds and eyes to see, the writing is plainly on the wall. Once again, a few examples must suffice. The glaciers of Alaska are a good case in point. Alaska is seven times bigger than the UK, and, according to *National Geographic*, has more glaciers than any other country in the world, estimated at around 100,000 in all, many in remote and inaccessible areas. Some of them are several thousand feet thick, cover hundreds of square miles, and are now indisputably suffering the effects of global warming. They are also said to be melting up to a hundred times faster than previously thought. Methane, a powerful

> **Forest areas the size of a football field have disappeared every minute.**

greenhouse gas, trapped under the ice and Arctic permafrost, is being released as the glaciers and ice fields melt and recede, contributing further to global warming and the consequent effects on biodiversity.

If climate change and global warming continue at present rates, sea levels in the Torres Strait Islands and even some areas along the east coast of Australia are projected to rise between six and ten metres in the foreseeable future. Some islands in the Torres Strait group, which have been inhabited for generations, have already been deserted; and graveyards in some have been opened up by rising tides and water levels. Climate change, with all its seen and unforeseen consequences, has been called 'the great moral dilemma of our time' and 'the outstanding threat' to life on earth as we know it. It is not hard to think that Peter would have warned the people of his day had these conditions prevailed then, or that he would have approved of doing so in these last days of the End Time.

In conclusion

In this closing chapter of *End Time People*, we have surveyed a wide range of evidence, in the form of fact and informed opinion, to substantiate the claim that what Peter wrote in the first century to people living in the last days is even more relevant and timely now than it was then. Even as Yeats could not have foreseen the extent of the moral slide into decadence in the twentieth century, neither could Peter have imagined how well his words would describe conditions that would prevail in the twenty-first century. We would all do well, then, to heed Peter's concluding advice to End Time people and let it shape our lives from this day forward:

> **'But the day of the Lord will come as a thief in the night, in which the heavens will pass away with a great noise, and the elements will melt with fervent heat; both the earth and the works that are in it will be burned up. Therefore, since all these things will be dissolved, *what manner of persons ought you to be in holy conduct and godliness?*'** (2 Peter 3:10, 11, emphasis supplied.)

What manner of people ought we to be? The question is pointed, pertinent, personal – and unavoidable. It requires an answer. Those who have read this book will know that Peter has already answered it, and that we may take courage and hope from what he has said. Yet to ignore the question amounts to denying it, a risk with eternal consequences that no honest, thinking, End Time believer can afford to take.

> **What manner of people ought we to be?**

For reflection and further study

How is Christ's life, death and resurrection the guarantee that He will return one day? In the era of Earth's 'climate emergency', geo-political turbulence, and moral and social decay, what does it mean to live 'expectantly'?

Sources

Reference works
Alexander, David and Pat, *The Lion Handbook to the Bible*
Bromiley, Geoffrey, *Theological Dictionary of the New Testament*
Ferguson, S. B. and Wright, D. F., eds., *New Dictionary of Theology*
Furness, J. M., *Vital Words of the Bible*
Ramseyer, J. P., *The Vocabulary of the Bible*
Renn, Stephen, ed., *Expository Dictionary of Bible Words*
Richardson, Alan, ed., *A Dictionary of Christian Theology*
  A Theological Word Book of the Bible
Souter, Alexander, *A Pocket Lexicon to the Greek New Testament*
Tulloch, Sara, ed., *The Reader's Digest Oxford Complete Wordfinder*
Young, Robert, *Analytical Concordance to the Holy Bible*
Von Allmen, J. J., ed., *Vocabulary of the Bible*

Commentaries
Barclay, William, *The Daily Study Bible*
Clowney, Edmund, *The Message of 1 Peter*
Green, Michael, *2 Peter and Jude*
Grudem, Wayne, *The First Epistle of Peter*
  Tyndale New Testament Commentary
Lenski, R. C. H., *The Interpretation of the Epistles of Peter*

Other works
Anderson, J. N. D., *Law and Grace*
Anderson, Norman, *God's Law and God's Love*
Arnold, Thomas, *The History of Rome*
Atkinson, James, *Justification by Faith*
Ball, Bryan W., *A Great Expectation*
  Grounds for Assurance and Hope
  Living in the Spirit
  ed., *The Essential Jesus*
  ed., *In the Beginning*
Beeke, J. R. and Pedersen, R. J., *Meet the Puritans*
Berkouwer, G. C., *Faith and Sanctification*
  The Return of Christ
Blamires, Harry, *The Christian Mind*
Bork, Robert H., *Slouching Towards Gomorrah*
Bright, John, *The Kingdom of God*
Bruinsma, Reinder, *He Comes: Why, When and How Jesus Christ Will Return*
Buchanan, James, *The Office and Work of the Holy Spirit*
Bunyan, John, *Grace Abounding to the Chief of Sinners*
  Pilgrim's Progress
Chadwick, Samuel, *The Call to Christian Perfection*
Colquhoun, Frank, *The Meaning of the Cross*
Dunton, Hugh, *Biblical Versions: A Consumer's Guide to the Bible*

Sources

Durant, John, *The Salvation of the Saints*
Goodspeed, E. J., *An Introduction to the New Testament*
Graham, Billy, *The Holy Spirit*
Green, Michael, *I Believe in the Holy Spirit*
　　The Empty Cross of Jesus
Griffin, William, *C. S. Lewis: The Authentic Voice*
Hess, Richard and Tsumara, David, *I Studied Inscriptions from Before the Flood*
Hobbes, Thomas, *Leviathan*
Kendall, R. T., ed., *The Word of the Lord*
Kevan, Ernest F., *The Grace of Law*
　　Keep His Commandments
Ladd, G. E., *A Theology of the New Testament*
LaRondelle, Hans, *Christ Our Salvation*
Lewis, C. S., *The Four Loves*
Lewontin, Richard, *Billions and Billions of Demons*
Lowe, Harry, *Redeeming Grace*
Mascall, E. L., *The Secularisation of Christianity*
Miller, Perry, *Errand into the Wilderness*
Morgan, G. Campbell, *The Parables and Metaphors of Our Lord*
Moore, A. L., *The Parousia in the New Testament*
Morris, Leon, *The Apostolic Preaching of the Cross*
Murray, John, *Redemption Accomplished and Applied*
Newbigin, Lesslie, *Sin and Salvation*
Pelikan, Jaroslav, *The Christian Intellectual*
Schaeffer, Francis, *The Church Before the Watching World*
　　Escape from Reason
　　The Mark of the Christian
Schnackenburg, Rudolf, *Christ – Present and Coming*
Shute, Neville, *On the Beach*
Smith, George A., *Historical Geography of the Holy Land*
Stott, John, *Christian Basics*
　　The Cross of Christ
　　Your Mind Matters
Sulpicius Severus, *Chronicles*
Tacitus, *Annals*
Travis, Stephen, *I Believe in the Second Coming of Christ*
　　The Jesus Hope
Warren, Max, *I Believe in the Great Commission*
Wells, David, *No Place for Truth*
Whitcomb, J. C. and Morris, H. M., *The Genesis Flood*
White, Ellen G., *The Desire of Ages*
　　The Great Controversy Between Christ and Satan